GLOBETROTTER™

Travel Guide

AMSTERDAM

D1354711

HOLLAND

NEW
HOLLAND

★★★ Highly recommended
★★ Recommended
★ See if you can

This edition first published in 2001
by New Holland Publishers (UK) Ltd
London • Cape Town • Sydney • Auckland
First edition published in 1996
10 9 8 7 6 5 4 3 2 1

Garfield House, 86 Edgware Road
London W2 2EA
United Kingdom

80 McKenzie Street
Cape Town 8001
South Africa

14 Aquatic Drive
Frenchs Forest, NSW 2086
Australia

218 Lake Road
Northcote, Auckland
New Zealand

Distributed in the USA by
The Globe Pequot Press
Connecticut

ISBN 1 84330 146 6

Manager Globetrotter Maps: John Loubser
Managing Editor: Thea Grobbelaar
Editors: Melany McCallum, Thea Grobbelaar,
Donald Reid, Catherine Randall
Design and DTP: Laurence Lemmon-Warde,
Kathryn Fotheringham
Picture Researcher: Emily Hedges
Cartographers: Nicole Engeler, Desireé Oosterberg
Compiler/Verifier: Genené Hart

Reproduction by Hirt & Carter (Pty) Ltd, Cape Town
Printed and bound in Hong Kong by Sing Cheong
Printing Co. Ltd.

Photographic Credits:
The Bridgeman Art Library, pages 62, 81;
Terry Harris, page 89;
Life File/Mike Maidment, page 111;
Life File/Andrew Ward, page 106;
The Mansell Collection, pages 11 (bottom), 16, 17;
Picture Bank Photo Library (PBPL), pages 19 (top),
34, 39, 46, 51, 71;
PBPL/Adrian Baker, pages 6, 21, 22, 84, 95, 96, 97, 98;
PBPL/Peter Baker, pages 40, 102;
Robert Harding Picture Library (RHPL), pages 10,
24 (top), 37, 43, 44 (top left), 49, 64, 74, 76, 77, 83, 109;
RHPL/Nigel Blythe, page 44 (top right);
RHPL/Philip Craven, pages 36, 56, 57;
RHPL/Roy Rainford, title page, pages 4, 7, 52, 58, 112;
RHPL/Phil Robinson, pages 104, 103;
RHPL/Michael Short, pages 13, 20, 66;
RHPL/I Vanderharst, page 92;
RHPL/Paul van Riel, pages 26, 29 (top), 41, 42, 45,
49, 50 (bottom), 63, 82;
RHPL/Adam Woolfitt, pages 8, 12, 15, 23, 24
(bottom), 25, 28, 32, 61, 65, 68, 75 (top);
Neil Setchfield, cover;
Jeroen Snÿders, pages 11, 19 (bottom), 38, 53, 54,
55 (top and bottom), 67, 80;
Travel Ink/Nick Battersby, page 14;
Travel Ink/Trevor Creighton, page 107;
Travel Ink/Abbie Enock, pages 9, 18, 29 (bottom),
30, 31, 50 (top), 52, 72, 73, 75 (bottom), 85, 86;
Travel Ink/David Toase, pages 27, 78, 98, 99, 100, 105.

Although every effort has been made to ensure
accuracy of facts, telephone and fax numbers in this
book, the publishers will not be held responsible for
changes that occur at the time of going to press.

Cover: *The Singel, the oldest and innermost of
Amsterdam's canal rings.*
Title page: *A beautifully lit bridge over the
Keizersgracht canal.*

CONTENTS

1
Introducing Amsterdam

Amsterdam is a city where the land meets the sea, old meets new, and bohemian lifestyles rub shoulders with hard-headed commercialism and bourgeois respectability. A rich cultural heritage combines with a lively dynamism to make this small but cosmopolitan capital one of the most popular of European destinations every year, drawing millions of visitors from all over the world.

It is a city of rich variety, from the gentrified **Jordaan** district to the bustling city centre and the narrow streets of the **Old Side**, where medieval churches look down on the gaudy neon of the raffish **red light district**. It can also boast picturesque old canalside homes, houseboats, tulip-filled parks, tree-lined waterways and superb museums unmatched in Europe.

Amsterdam is not a big city; it has about 725,000 residents, but few cities are so easy to explore. The determined sightseer can pack most if not all of Amsterdam's museums, art galleries and historic buildings into one busy weekend; that said, the city offers greater rewards to those who have the opportunity to take it at an easier pace.

Amsterdam is something of a newcomer among the great cities of Europe. Unlike Paris, Rome, or London it came into its own little more than three centuries ago, and most of the buildings and monuments you will see as you explore are even more recent than that. Despite its small size, its position at the mouth of Europe's mightiest river has given it an important role to play.

NORTH SEA
(NOORDZEE)

NETHER-
LANDS

UNITED
KINGDOM   Amsterdam

GERMANY

BELGIUM

FRANCE

TOP ATTRACTIONS

*** Rijksmuseum: superb collection of paintings by the great Dutch masters, plus a vast array of other works.
*** Rijksmuseum Vincent Van Gogh: world's finest collection of Van Gogh's work.
** Stedelijk Museum: always changing exhibits of striking contemporary artists.
** Westerkerk: the prettiest church in the city, with fine views from its tower.
* Amsterdam Maritime Museum: reconstructions of the elegant sailing ships.

Opposite: *Houseboats line the Brouwersgracht canal.*

Below: *Bulb fields colour
the countryside in spring.*

THE LAND

Amsterdam stands on the estuary of the River **IJ**, close
to its mouth on the landlocked **IJsselmeer** and about
20km (12½ miles) from the North Sea coast. Until the
1950s, IJsselmeer, then known as the Zuider Zee, was
an open bight of the North Sea; it was then dammed
to allow land reclamation and its taming is one of the
great triumphs of the Dutch in their centuries-long
battle with the sea.

Since its foundation, Amsterdam has been shaped by
this stubborn struggle with the water around it. Although
the sea has brought prosperity, first from fishing and then
from trade and a far-flung overseas empire, it has contin-
ually threatened to overwhelm the city and the farmland
around it. The battle has lasted centuries, and continues
today, although even in an era when threats of rising sea
levels due to global warming are voiced, it seems unlikely
that the sea will ever gain the upper hand.

It has come close: at the time of the founding of
Amsterdam much of modern Holland, the province
which surrounds the city, was swamp or seabed and
over the years great floods have sometimes threatened
the city and its hinterland. But the stubborn and ingenious Dutch, over centuries,
pushed the sea back. With the introduction
of steam-powered pumps in the 19th century the tide finally turned in favour of
the city and the last inland seas – such as
the Harlemmermeer, where Amsterdam
Schiphol Airport now stands – were
drained to create reclaimed farmlands
called polders.

In a sense, Amsterdam turned its back
on the sea in the late 19th century. The
broad estuary of the IJ is now hidden
behind the grandiose frontage of the
Centraal Station and its surrounding office
blocks, and the first-time visitor may not
realize that a major port lies within a few
hundred metres of the city centre.

Left: *A canal cruise is one of the best ways to see Amsterdam.*

City Profile

The wide river IJ, hidden from sight from the city centre by the façade of Centraal Station, separates central Amsterdam from a handful of residential suburbs on the north shore. Along the south bank of the IJ are the city's docklands. Concentric, semi-circular rings of canals spread south from the IJ, dividing central Amsterdam – the city's commercial and touristic heart – from an outer crescent of mainly residential suburbs. Still further to the south and west, separated from the city proper by a multi-lane ring road, are Amsterdam's industrial and commercial areas.

Amsterdam's historic heart is a semi-circular shape, enclosed by the canals that link the **River Amstel**, flowing into the city from the south, with the IJ, which forms central Amsterdam's northern edge. The oldest part of the city is enclosed by the ring of the **Singel** canal on the south and west and by the **Kloveniers Burgwal** canal on the east. Moving out from the city centre are newer canal rings: the **Herengracht**, **Keizersgracht** and **Prinsengracht**, built in the city's 17th-century Golden Age to accommodate its fast-growing population. The semi-circular **Singelgracht** forms the outer boundary of central Amsterdam.

A DAY'S WALK

To take in Amsterdam's highlights in a full day's walking, walk from **Brouwersgracht** down Prinsengracht to the **Noorderkerk**. Crossing the Prinsenstraat bridge, walk down the east bank to **Anne Frank Huis** and **Westerkerk**. A detour along Raadhuisstraat takes you to the **Royal Palace**. From here take Nieuwezijds Voorburgwal to the **Amsterdam Historical Museum**, the **Begijnhof** and the **Spui**, crossing the Singel to visit the **Bloemenmarkt**. Walk south on Leidsestraat, cross the **Herengracht** and walk along the south bank to Nieuwe Spiegelstraat, then down the Spiegelgracht and across the Lijnbaangracht and Singelgracht canals to reach **Museumplein**, site of the **Van Gogh Museum** and the **Rijksmuseum**.

Above: *Flower-filled window boxes brighten a Noordermarkt gable.*

The canals, originally built to drain marshy land, have become Amsterdam's major feature. Building land has always been in short supply, so houses are squeezed side by side along the canals. Buildings are narrow, five or six storeys high, and set on a foundation of piles driven through the soft surface to firmer ground below. Many older buildings lean drunkenly against their neighbours as their foundations subside with time.

Brick was and is the preferred building material, and has dominated Amsterdam's architecture from the wealthy merchants' homes of the 16th and 17th centuries to the grand façades of the 19th-century Centraal Station and the imposing Rijksmuseum on Museumplein.

Although the inner city is intensely urban, just outside the centre wider recreational spaces are provided by the elegantly landscaped **Vondelpark**, the **Hortus Botanicus** gardens and other patches of urban greenery. In the centre itself, the canals provide some visual relief, particularly in summer when every apartment dweller makes up for the lack of a garden with window boxes full of flowers.

The Randstad Towns

Within a 60km (37 mile) radius of Amsterdam lie the towns collectively called the Randstad (Round City). An excellent road and rail network means none of these is more than 45 minutes away from Amsterdam, and many of them are well worth a half- or full-day excursion from the city. **The Hague** is the diplomatic and political capital of the Netherlands, with a rich heritage of historic buildings and museums; **Rotterdam**, the Netherlands' second biggest city, displays some of the most striking of post-war architecture in Europe; and **Haarlem**, **Utrecht**, **Leiden**, **Delft** and **Gouda** all have picturesque medieval centres.

Climate

Amsterdam has a northern European climate with four distinct seasons. **Summer**, from June to September, can be warm, but cool and rainy weather is always a possibility. **Autumn** is a cool and misty season, giving way in October to increasingly cold, wet and windy winter weather. The nearby North Sea always makes its presence felt, and while the city is close to sea level, sub-zero **winter** temperatures in the centre are not all that uncommon. From November to March the thermometer is rarely far off freezing point, and Amsterdam's canals when frozen and snow-covered are every bit as pretty as in spring and summer. **Spring**, in April and May, is one of the most popular times to visit Amsterdam and the Netherlands, with trees along the canals springing into new leaf and the famous bulb fields in brilliant bloom.

Above: *Bicycles and tulips are twin symbols of Amsterdam.*

AMSTERDAM	J	F	M	A	M	J	J	A	S	O	N	D
AVERAGE TEMP. °C	4	5	9	14	19	21	22	22	18	13	9	5
AVERAGE TEMP. °F	32	41	48	57	66	70	72	72	64	55	48	41
Hours of sun daily	2	2	3	4	4	6	7	7	7	4	3	2
Days of rainfall	20	15	15	15	15	15	15	15	15	20	25	20
RAINFALL mm	76	50	50	52	55	60	80	80	85	87	90	75
RAINFALL in	3	2	2	2	2.1	2.4	3.1	3.1	3.3	3.4	3.5	3

EARLY AMSTERDAM

The first record of a settlement where Amsterdam now stands is in the annals of Floris V, Count of Holland, dating from 1275, which mention the grant of free passage on all the waterways in the region to the burghers of Aemstelle Dam. It was not until 30 years later, however, that Amsterdam received a town charter. By that time the town had its first fortifications, a series of moats around the city. The mud dredged out to form these moats was heaped on the inner bank to form a solid rampart or *dijk*. None of these survive, but streetnames indicate the location of these early city walls – Zeedijk (Sea Wall), Nieuwendijk (New Wall) and Haarlemmerdijk (Haarlem Wall).

Below: *One of the city's hidden nooks, the Begijnhof.*

HISTORY IN BRIEF

Throughout its 800-year history, Amsterdam has always been the driving force behind the stubbornly independent and fiercely democratic Netherlands. In turn, this relatively tiny country has had an influence on modern European history and culture significantly out of proportion to the size of its territory and population.

In prehistoric and Roman times, and into the early Middle Ages, the site on which Amsterdam now stands was empty marshland between the North Sea and the estuaries of the IJ and Amstel rivers. Later it became a small fishing settlement, but by the early 13th century the original village of **Aemstelle Dam** – the dam on the Amstel – had grown into a prosperous small mercantile town, the commercial centre of the lands of the Bishops of Utrecht, who in 1313 ceded the territory to the Count of Holland.

City of Traders

Throughout the Middle Ages Amsterdam wrangled with a series of rulers and rivals to keep and extend its trading privileges and enlarge its web of trade routes. The sea gave Amsterdam a highway to ports all over Europe and the rivers carried its trade goods far inland. Through the Middle Ages Amsterdam's prosperity was boosted by commerce first with other North Sea ports, then with the powerful **Hanseatic League** of Baltic trading cities, and eventually even further afield. By the mid-15th century it had become the most important port in northern Europe, trading across the length and breadth of the mighty Holy Roman Empire, whose dynastic lands included all of what is now the Netherlands, Belgium, Germany, Austria, Switzerland and the Czech Republic. In 1489 the **Emperor Maximilian I** granted Amsterdam the royal seal and his personal protection, bolstering the city's sturdy independent mindedness. With a population of 9000, the city was one of the biggest, wealthiest and most important in 15th-century Europe.

Reformation

However, stormy times lay ahead for the Netherlands, and indeed all of Europe. The ships and barges that brought Amsterdam's sea and river trade also brought the new thinking of the Reformation. The radical ideas of reformers such as Martin Luther, Erasmus and Calvin were quickly taken up by the traditionally free-thinking and tolerant Dutch and the Netherlands became a refuge for Protestants from less liberal parts of the continent. In 1522 Emperor Charles V introduced the fanatical **Inquisition** on the Netherlands to quell the forces of the Reformation and restore the Catholic orthodoxy. In the next 30 years some 30,000 people were executed for their Protestant beliefs, but the savagery of the Inquisition still failed to bring the provinces of the Netherlands back into the Catholic fold.

Above: *Medieval weighhouse at St Antoniespoort.*
Left: *Through their active involvement in sea trade, it was inevitable that the Dutch would come into conflict with other nations.*

The Struggle for Independence

Dissidence turned to armed resistance in 1568, following the brutal occupation of Amsterdam by the Spanish **Duke of Alva** and the execution of the Dukes of Egmont and Hoorn, leaders of the Protestant cause. For the next six years, Spanish commanders attempted with great brutality to snuff out resistance by the 'Beggars', as the Dutch rebels were nicknamed. Ill-equipped and ill-trained, the rebels were no match for Alva's seasoned veterans in the field, but under the leadership of **Prince William of Orange** (known as 'William the Silent') they fought a guerrilla campaign by land and sea. Protestant resistance to Spain was strongest in the northern provinces, while the southern Netherlands – present-day Belgium – remained strongly Catholic.

Throughout these upheavals, Amsterdam remained solidly pro-Spanish, and its mainly Catholic ruling clique made a healthy profit supplying the occupying forces. In 1578, however, with Spanish power suddenly on the wane, the city's rulers pragmatically decided to make their peace with William. The Catholic party was driven from power by its Protestant rivals and in 1581 the united northern provinces of the Netherlands formally renounced all allegiance to Spain, declaring themselves a republic ruled by the **States General**, to be made up of representative of each of the seven provinces, called advocates, and the Stadhouder, William (the Silent) of Orange.

William was assassinated by a Catholic fanatic on 10 July 1584, but although hostilities with Spain were to continue intermittently for the next 80 years, Dutch independence was firmly established. A series of defeats on land and sea forced the Spaniards to sign a 12-year truce in 1609.

UNSPOKEN HERO

William the Silent, Prince of the House of Orange and the first Stadhouder of the free Netherlands, earned his nickname by his reluctance to come out for the Protestant cause until 1568, when he led the first campaign against the Spanish Duke of Alva, beginning the Eighty Years War against Spain. Ten years later his rebel army and fleet had driven the Spaniards out of the Netherlands – Amsterdam was the last city to surrender to him – and he was chosen by the States General (the governing council) to be the newly independent country's first Stadhouder.

The Golden Age

The overthrow of Spanish rule ushered in a new era for Amsterdam. Even while the wars of independence went on the city grew: in the middle of the 16th century it had approximately 14,000 inhabitants, and by the mid-17th century this had grown to over 200,000. Amsterdam's tolerance attracted refugees from all over Europe, including German Lutherans, French Huguenots, Sephardic Jews from the Spanish lands and Ashkenazi Jews from eastern Europe. These refugees brought with them new skills, trade contacts and investment. The city became a haven for painters such as **Rembrandt** and **Vermeer** and the philosophers **Spinoza**, **Descartes** and **Lipsius**. Religious tolerance was also extended to those Dutch Catholics who chose not to renounce their faith. The great city churches became Protestant places of worship and Catholics were barred from practising their faith openly, but several 'secret' Catholic churches still flourished, with some congregations numbering into hundreds and even thousands.

While much of northern Europe suffered from the effects of the **Thirty Years War** (1618–48), the Dutch Republic seized every advantage. Its well-armed and disciplined troops proved a match for anything sent against them, and throughout the 17th century it was the greatest naval power in the world.

By the mid-17th century the city had already taken on its modern form, thanks to the foresight of its planners. Work began as early as 1613 on the three canal rings – the Herengracht, Keizersgracht and Prinsengracht – which today separate historic Amsterdam

---

DECADES OF WAR

For a century and a half after taking up arms against Spain, the Netherlands was at war more often than not. Defying powerful enemies on both land and sea, the new Dutch republic flourished.
1568–1648 At war with Spain, and from 1618, with the Holy Roman Empire.
1651–53 War with England.
1689–91 ·Involved in civil war in United Kingdom.
1701–14 War of Spanish Succession against France.

Opposite: *William the Silent, leader of the Dutch independence struggle.*
Below: *The Montelbaans toren, subject of studies by Rembrandt.*

OVERSEAS EMPIRE

The Eighty Years War gave the Dutch a fine pretext to seize from Spain's vassal, Portugal, the ports and territories established by 16th-century Portuguese navigators all through Africa and Asia. Establishing a strong base on the Cape of Good Hope, Dutch admirals occupied Mauritius (naming it after their own Prince Maurice) and drove the Portuguese from Ceylon (Sri Lanka) and Malacca. The jewel of the Dutch empire in Asia was Batavia (now Jakarta), founded in 1619, from which Dutch power spread throughout the islands of the East Indies.

from its outer suburbs. Merchants made rich by the lucrative Baltic grain trade had luxurious townhouses built along the new canals and their wealth trickled down to painters and craftsmen. The elite commissioned Rembrandt and his peers, but ordinary folk could afford the cheaper work of hacks of the artists' guild and by 1650 more than 2.5 million paintings hung on Dutch walls. Visitors were awed by the city's prosperity, clean streets and public works; by 1670, when cities like London and Paris were mostly sewage-scented slums, Amsterdam boasted streets lit each night by 2000 oil lanterns.

Right: *The Schreierstoren with the St Nikolaas Kerk in the background.*
Opposite: *The East India Company's merchantmen brought riches from Asia.*

Eastern Adventure

The Eighty Years War with Spain closed the ports of Spain and Portugal to Dutch traders, who promptly set out to forge their own trade routes to both east and west. In 1595 **Cornelis de Houtman** launched an expedition to break the Spanish-Portuguese monopoly of the trade routes to the East Indies, where untold wealth awaited any merchant who brought home a cargo of pepper, cloves or other spices. De Houtman made two successful voyages and a stampede to get into the Eastern trade began. In 1602 the rival merchants – with the hard-headed common sense typical of Amsterdammers to this day – agreed to stop cutting each other's throats. Instead, they formed the **United East India Company** (Vereinigde Oostindische Compagnie) to control and protect their enterprise in Asia.

With its own powerful navy and army to protect its ships and factories, the VOC was enormously influential and incredibly wealthy. Overseas, it was in effect the Dutch government, with the rights of a sovereign power. At home, its bottomless coffers made Amsterdam the supreme power among the cities and provinces of the young Dutch Republic. A chain of Dutch colonies stretched from Amsterdam to the Far East, and the flags of the VOC and the Dutch Republic flew over the Cape of Good Hope, Mauritius, Colombo, Batavia (now Jakarta), Malacca and even as far as Nagasaki.

Meanwhile, the less successful **West India Company** carried Dutch colours west to the Caribbean and the Americas. Under the company's auspices, an English adventurer named Henry Hudson explored the eastern seaboard of North America, discovering the river which still bears his name and founding the settlement of New Amsterdam – now New York. However, much of the wealth of the West India Company came from a trade much more evil than spice: the slave trafficking between West Africa and the Caribbean.

BORN TRADERS

In its famous Golden Age Amsterdam became the world's leading entrepot for trade in all the **spices** and aromatics of the East – cloves, cinnamon, pepper and nutmeg – as well as for **tea**, **coffee**, **sugar** from Brazil and the Caribbean and **tobacco** from the Americas. In earlier centuries the city traded in less fragrant commodities. Its earliest fortunes were built on **salt cod** and **whale oil** from Scandinavia, **beer** from Hamburg, **tar**, **wool** and **coal**, and **herring** from the North Sea fisheries. Amsterdam's location enabled it to trade with the major ports of the Baltic, the North Sea, the Mediterranean and the Atlantic as well as with the river ports of central Europe.

Above: *In the mid-17th century the Dutch fleet ruled from the North Sea to the Indian Ocean.*
Opposite: *Louis Bonaparte, ill-fated King of the Netherlands.*

ROYAL FAMILY

The Dutch take their 'citizen monarchy' for granted, celebrating the Queen's Birthday with a day of open-air entertainment but investing their royal family with far less pomp and circumstance than surrounds the British House of Windsor (to whom Dutch Queen Beatrix is related through her great grandmother, Queen Victoria).

Revolution, Invasion and Monarchy

Wars with England and France followed in the 17th and 18th centuries, but the Dutch held their own surprisingly well considering the might of their opponents. In the war of 1666–7 the Dutch fleet under Admirals **De Ruyter** and **Van Tromp** proved far superior to the English, and in a second war from 1672–8, the Dutch held off both England and France.

In 1688, with the overthrow of the unpopular King James II of England, Stadhouder **William III**, husband of James's daughter Mary, was invited to take the British throne. He ruled jointly with his wife until her death in 1694, and then alone until his own death in 1702.

Alliance with England involved the Netherlands in wars with France from 1688–97, the War of the Spanish Succession (1702–13) and the Seven Years War (1756–63). These sapped the country's energies and drained its coffers. New Amsterdam was lost to the English, and the Golden Age drew to a close.

Amsterdam, however, remained prosperous, becoming one of Europe's most important financial centres and generating almost a quarter of the Republic's entire income. Political power remained in the hands of the Stadhouder, theoretically an elected national leader but in practice a hereditary prince of the House of Orange, who was frequently at loggerheads with the council of regents drawn from the country's wealthy and powerful families. By the mid-18th century a newly prosperous middle and professional class, shut out of this cumbersome duopoly, began to demand its share of political power. The more moderate allied themselves with the Stadhouder, while the more radical called for a truly democratic constitution.

Towards the end of the 18th century, revolutionaries calling themselves the **Patriots** tried to overthrow the ruling oligarchy, only to be driven into exile in France. Not long afterwards they were back, this time backed by the eager troops of the new French Republic, who overthrew the government of the Stadhouder and the States General and declared a Batavian Republic. This was soon swept away by French Emperor **Napoleon Bonaparte**, who set up his brother, **Louis**, as King of the Netherlands.

The results of this incorporation into the Bonapartist empire were far from positive, however. Britain, which had long looked on the Dutch as dangerous commercial and naval rivals, took the opportunity to seize most of the VOC's eastern possessions and Malacca, Ceylon, Mauritius and the Cape were lost for good. The Netherlands languished under French rule until 1813, when, with the Bonaparte star waning, the Stadhouder **William V** returned to make himself King William I over an expanded Netherlands. The new kingdom included the southern provinces (now Belgium) for the first time. The union did not, however, last very long; in 1831–2 the southern provinces rose in revolt and Belgium became an independent kingdom.

WINDMILLS

Some 140 windmills were in use throughout the Netherlands in 1765, according to contemporary tax records, but only a handful survive. Windmills are first mentioned in Amsterdam's records as early as 1307, and provided power not only to pump the polders dry but to grind grain, saw wood, and run many other industrial processes. As windmill design grew more sophisticated their sails were designed to set themselves automatically against the wind. Wind power was gradually supplanted by steam, then by diesel, though Dutch engineers have helped pioneer the use of high-tech wind generators as a 'green' source of electrical power.

The 19th Century

Through the early 19th century Amsterdam and the
Netherlands became a backwater, and only in the latter
part of the century was the economy revitalized. The age
of steam made Amsterdam a vital link between Europe's
railway networks and transatlantic liner and freight
services, while wealth poured into the city from the newly
discovered South African diamond mines. It was almost a
second Golden Age, and many of Amsterdam's public
buildings, including the Rijksmuseum, Centraal Station,
the Beurs and others, date from this era. Overseas, the
Dutch continued to expand their empire in the East Indies,
bringing most of what is now Indonesia under their control. In the 1870s, the VOC's monopoly was ended and
private investment in the colonies was allowed, opening
up a new flow of trade.

Right: *The Rijksmuseum
houses one of the world's
finest art collections.*

Occupation and Liberation

During **World War I** the Netherlands sensibly managed to remain neutral, thus escaping the disasters which overwhelmed the rest of Europe. During **World War II** the Dutch were not given this option. In May 1940 Germany invaded, taking only five days to occupy the country. The following year Japan launched its assault on the Dutch East Indies. By early 1941 the occupiers had begun rounding up Amsterdam's Jewish citizens (many of whom had fled there earlier from Germany) for transportation to concentration camps in Germany and Poland. In a remarkable expression of solidarity with their fellow citizens, Amsterdam dockworkers launched a protest strike on 25–26 February 1941. It was ruthlessly crushed.

Underground resistance groups and individuals helped to shelter Jews and others in hiding. As late as 1944 – and despite the savage German reprisals against strikers – Dutch railwaymen went on strike. In revenge, the Germans cut off food supplies, leading to widespread famine, still remembered as the 'Hunger Winter'. Allied troops liberated the Netherlands in May 1945, arriving in Amsterdam on 4 May, only a few days before the German surrender and the end of the war in Europe.

Above: *The monument on the Dam Square commemorates martyrs of the German occupation.*
Below: *Memorial to the striking dockworkers of 1941.*

Above: *The Dutch Royal Guard presents arms outside the Palace.*
Opposite: *Open-air cafés are an attractive part of the Amsterdam summer scene.*

Modern Amsterdam

The end of World War II brought in a period of re-evaluation for the Netherlands. A misguided attempt to hold on to the East Indies ended with the independence of Indonesia in 1949, and Amsterdam turned its back on the colonial era to become one of Europe's most forward looking cities.

New, fast motorway links were built to connect it with the rest of the Netherlands and Europe, and the founding of the European Economic Community tied the country firmly into a flourishing new economic order. From being a prosperous but rather inward looking city, more concerned with overseas trade than with its continental neighbours, Amsterdam stepped forward to take its place at the heart of European affairs.

HISTORICAL CALENDAR

c.1000AD Earliest settlements around the Amstel.
1317 Amsterdam granted to William, Count of Holland.
1428 Amsterdam comes under rule of Duke of Burgundy.
1477 Amsterdam passes under rule of Holy Roman Emperor.
1489 Maximilian grants the city right to carry the imperial crown on its coat of arms.
1517 Protestant Reformation begins in Germany; ideas soon popular in Amsterdam.
1566 Protestant iconoclasts smash statues and burn churches. Philip II of Spain sends 10,000 troops under Duke of Alva to Netherlands.
1578 Amsterdam yields to William the Silent.

1581 Northern provinces renounce allegiance to Spain and declare republic ruled by the States General and the Stadhouder, William (the Silent) of Orange.
1584 William assassinated. Maurice of Nassau becomes the Stadhouder.
1602 Dutch East India Company formed.
1609 12 Years Truce signed with Spain, recognizing Dutch independence and ushering in Amsterdam's Golden Age.
1795 French Revolutionary army occupies Netherlands with widespread popular support.
1806 Napoleon places younger brother Louis Bonaparte on throne of Netherlands.

1813 French withdrawal; Netherlands becomes Kingdom under William I.
1872–6 Building of North Sea Canal revives city's sea trade.
1940–5 German occupation.
1940s–50s Netherlands loses overseas empire. Completion of Zuider Zee reclamation.
1960s–70s Liberal city regime attracts artists and bohemians.
1980s Squatters oppose demolition of housing in city centre.
1987 Completion of controversial Stopera complex.
1997 NewMetropolis Science and Technology Centre opens.
2001 Amsterdam municipality legitimizes gay 'marriages', and Netherlands legalizes euthanasia.

Politically, the post World War II decades have been dominated by pragmatic, moderate governments, and Amsterdammers have enjoyed some of the most comprehensive social welfare, health and education benefits in Europe. **Tourism** – attracted first by the city's treasury of fine arts, later by its laid-back lifestyle – has become steadily more important and Amster-

dam attracts more than 20 million visitors every year. New building has been carried out in the second half of the 20th century, but there has also been much restoration of sub-standard housing and important public buildings. In the 1960s, Amsterdam became a magnet for the hippy culture of Europe, who were attracted by a liberal city government prepared to turn a blind eye to youthful excess.

Amsterdam's traditional tolerance of different faiths, as long as they were discreetly practiced, finds expression in a modern-day liberalism which some believe has gone too far. A relaxed approach to pornography means hard-core porn openly on display next to more innocuous picture postcards. Legislation of prostitution has given the city one of Europe's most lurid red-light districts. An open-minded attitude to homosexuality has made the city a gay Mecca. Decriminalizing soft drug use has made the city the cannabis capital of Europe. Amsterdam has also become a cosmopolitan city. Many immigrants from Turkey, Greece, North Africa, Indonesia, Surinam (formerly Dutch Guyana) and the Antilles swell the city's workforce and now account for about 30% of its population.

'COFFEE SHOPS'

Amsterdam has long had a liberal attitude towards soft drug use. Possession of cannabis resin (hash) or marijuana (grass) is not legal but the authorities long ago gave up prosecuting discreet users. In euphemistically named 'coffee shops' customers can choose any of a dozen types of mind-expanding substances to enjoy at home or over a cup of coffee on the premises. There are about 450 'coffee shops' in Amsterdam, 180 of them in the inner city. As a result of this policy, cannabis users are less likely to come into contact with hard drugs, and the Netherlands has a much lower rate of hard drug addiction than many other countries with much tougher regimes.

BICYCLES

Amsterdam boasts 550,000 bicycles – more than one per household. Ranks of bikes stand padlocked outside Centraal Station every day, and on Amsterdam's flat streets they are a quiet, effortless and non-polluting way of getting around. You can rent bicycles by the day from a number of outlets in the city centre, and a bike is the ideal way to travel independently around the city centre.

GOVERNMENT AND ECONOMY

After throwing off the Spanish yoke in 1581, the Netherlands became the first nation since medieval Venice to experiment with a republican form of government. The monarchy, established in 1814, gradually became more democratically responsive, with constitutional reforms in 1848 limiting the power of the monarch and widening the franchise. Today, the Netherlands is a constitutional monarchy. The House of Orange, the dynasty founded by William the Silent, remains on the throne in the person of **Queen Beatrix**, who succeeded her mother, Queen Juliana, in 1980. The Dutch have a deep affection for their royal family, but the monarchy has no real political power and is surrounded with little of the pomp and ceremony of, for example, the British throne.

Executive and legislative power is in the hands of an elected prime minister and a two-chamber parliament which meets in **The Hague**, the political and diplomatic capital of the Netherlands. Amsterdam is governed by a mayor and city council and is located in North Holland, one of the 12 provinces of the Netherlands. The others are South Holland, Utrecht, Zeeland, Groningen, North Brabant, Drenthe, Limburg, Overijssel, Gelderland, Friesland, and Flevoland, a region of polder reclaimed from the IJsselmeer and declared a province in 1986.

The Netherlands is one of the founding members of the **European Economic Community** (now the **European Union**), has close economic ties with its European neighbours, and was among the first to join the single European currency, the euro, in 1999. The economy is mixed, with a substantial public sector balanced by

Below: *The Binnenhof in the Hague, seat of the first Dutch parliament.*

Above: *Europe's inland waterways meet the sea at busy Dutch ports.*

a long-standing commitment to free-market economics. The country remains committed to state involvement in providing health care, housing, education and social welfare for all. Housing, however, remains the most expensive in the European Union, because of the shortage of building land, and canal houseboats are still a popular alternative to land-based housing.

Set close to the heart of the European Union, with the major cities of Belgium, Germany, the UK and France less than an hour away by air, Amsterdam is a major **commercial** and **financial** centre. **Tourism** is also one of the city's bigger moneyspinners, with over 3 million foreign visitors annually. The administrative and service sectors, along with tourism, are the city's major employers. Rotterdam's vast Europoort complex is Europe's biggest seaport, both in area and in terms of tonnage handled, but Amsterdam is also a busy **shipping** centre.

Standards of living are high, with the Netherlands ranking as one of the most prosperous European nations. Outside the major cities, agriculture remains a major employer and earner of foreign currency. Dairy products, including the famed Dutch cheeses of Edam, Gouda and other regions, are important. The flower bulb industry, founded in the 16th and 17th centuries, is also a significant one.

STATISTICS
Amsterdam has:
3.25 million foreign visitors each year
725,000 inhabitants of **145** nationalities
600,000 bulb flowers in parks and public gardens
550,000 bicycles
220,000 trees
32,000 hotel beds
2400 houseboats
1402 cafés and bars
1281 bridges
240 city trams
206 paintings by Van Gogh
165 antique shops
160 canals
120 waterbikes
70 glass-topped boats
24 diamond polishing factories
22 paintings by Rembrandt.

AMSTERDAMMERS

The citizens of Amsterdam have a strong contrary streak which runs all the way back to the Reformation and beyond, finding expression in the frequent riots in the working-class Jordaan in the 19th century, the Dock-workers strike against the Nazis in February 1941, the 'provocations' of the prankster Provo movement in the hippy 60s and the occupations by militant squatters in the confrontational 80s.

Above: *Many locals use the canals for recreation.*
Below: *There's always somewhere to take the weight off your feet.*

THE PEOPLE

Tolerance, tradition and protest are all part of the city's character. Since the Middle Ages, Amsterdammers seem to have seen the benefits of tolerating almost anything which does not interfere with the important business of making money, combining a hard-headed approach to commerce and business with a remarkable willingness to experiment with new ideas. Thus, just as the city welcomed Protestants, Catholics and Jews in the 15th and 16th centuries, so it has taken a broad view of soft drug use, commercial sex, homosexuality and other tricky topics.

The Dutch character balances liberalism and conservatism. Traditions are respected, and there is a strong history of protest against injustice. The Netherlands has always been quick to dispense with governments which ignore the will of the people, from Philip II to the present day. Since the mid-1990s the national government has been left of centre, but Amsterdam's politics tend to be more radical and liberal than those of the country as a whole, with left-wingers controlling the city council even when centre-right national governments are in power.

During the 1980s and 90s there was considerable sympathy for the squatters' movement, which had grown out of two generations of youth protest and played a part in resisting the conversion of central Amsterdam from a living and working community into a sterile commercial district.

Women occupy a high proportion of seats in the Dutch parliament and on the Amsterdam city council and enjoy effective legal protection against exploitation at home and at work.

In 2001 the city council met acclaim from liberals and protest from conservatives when it voted to put homosexual relationships on the same legal basis as conventional marriages. Also in 2001, the Netherlands became the first country in Europe to legalize euthanasia. Amsterdam's tolerance extends to the tourist hordes who clutter streets and pavements year-round. The locals leave them to get on with their sightseeing while everyday life continues around them.

Above: *Thousands of locals get around by bicycle.*

Language

Dutch is closely related to German. Grammar and vocabulary are not hard for English-speakers to grasp, but the Dutch often find considerable amusement in foreigners' attempts to come to terms with the idiosyncratic vowels and consonants of their language. Learning how to pronounce place names can be tricky. Few visitors realize immediately that IJ and Spui both rhyme with 'eye'. Other sounds are easier. The double 'a' (as in *centraal* and *nationaal*) is pronounced just as it looks. Attempts to master a few basic phrases will always be appreciated, and a grasp of place name pronunciation will certainly help you to find your way around.

Failure to master the language need cause no problems, as virtually everyone in Amsterdam is competent in English. Tourist office literature, menus, maps and street signs are also produced in English and Amsterdam even has its own monthly English-language listings magazines, *Time Out* and *What's On in Amsterdam*. The city also has a number of English-language bookshops and an English language theatre, and most city-centre cinemas show English-language films undubbed. Museums and art galleries, too, display a wide range of information in English as well as in Dutch.

USEFUL WORDS

Finding your way around Amsterdam is easier if you understand at least some of the terminology used in naming streets and canals. Some of the most common terms are:

Gracht ● Canal
Kanaal ● Canal
Sluis ● Sluice-bridge
Dijk ● Dike or city wall
Wal ● Wall
Brug ● Bridge
Singel ● Moat
Kerk ● Church
Plein ● Square
Straat ● Street
Laan ● Avenue
Haven ● Harbour
Poort ● City gate
Noord ● North
Zuid ● South
Oost ● East
West ● West

Religion

With the wars of religion four centuries in the past, Dutch society is religiously tolerant, with few causes of friction between different communities. The country's **Christian** community remains very evenly divided. Catholic and Protestant believers each account for just over 40% of the population, with the remaining 20% from other faiths or non-denominational. In tune with the society around them, many of the Netherlands' Catholic clerics have frequently taken a much more liberal line than the Vatican on contentious issues such as abortion and contraception. Amsterdam's large **Jewish** community was drawn from the ranks of refugees first from 16th-century Spain and Portugal and later emigrants from eastern Europe and, in the 1930s, from Nazi Germany. During the German occupation of the city, more than 70,000 Jews were deported to concentration camps, and the Jewish community now numbers only a few thousand.

Art and Culture

Few cities anywhere can match Amsterdam's artistic heritage. The wealth of the city's 16th- and 17th-century merchant princes was not only reinvested in business and in gracious homes but went to patronize a generation of Europe's greatest painters, giving impetus to an artistic tradition that makes Amsterdam one of Europe's great centres of the visual arts even today.

Below: *Van Gogh's work adorns the city's fine museums and appear in the windows of every postcard-shop.*

The painters whose works hang in the city's fine museums – the **Brueghels**, **Frans Hals**, **Vermeer**, **Rembrandt**, **Piet Mondriaan** and **Vincent van Gogh**, to name just a few of the most renowned – are among the world's greatest. The city continues to provide inspiration and a home for new artists, and two leading schools of art, the **Rijksacademie** and the **Rietveld Academie**, are located in Amsterdam. Dutch government initiatives continue to support the visual arts – for example, the state can make interest-free loans to allow people to buy works by living Dutch artists. The best places to see the work of contemporary Amsterdam painters are the **Stedelijk Museum** (*see* p. 64), the **CoBrA museum** (*see* p. 91) and **Stichting de Appel**, at Nieuwe Speigelstraat 10 (open Tuesday–Sunday 12:00–17:00). For real enthusiasts, the annual **Kunst RAI** commercial exhibition, held in Amsterdam's RAI centre, is a must, with works by Europe's leading artists on sale.

Above: *The Rijksmuseum, a treasury of great art.*

Architecture

Since the Golden Age of the 16th and 17th centuries, Amsterdam has produced some of Europe's most striking architecture. During the city's 16th-century flourishing, architect **Hendrik de Keyser** gave it fine churches and mansions, and his successors added to the city's heritage year by year. However, Amsterdam's glories are on a much smaller and more human scale than those of older, grander European cities. There are no great cathedrals or palaces to compare with Notre Dame, St Peter's or Versailles, and certainly no ancient relics to match the Colosseum or the Acropolis.

Making up for the lack of such grand vistas, however, are the hundreds of tidy, doll's house-like homes, with their characteristic painted shutters and decorative gables, which line Amsterdam's canals. Two of the most striking buildings in the city are the **Centraal Station** and the **Rijksmuseum**, both in red brick and designed by **P.J.H. Cuypers** (1827–1921). The innovative and adventurous Cuypers gave the Netherlands a number of striking neo-Gothic churches and other public buildings.

REVIVING DOCKLANDS

Some of Amsterdam's trendiest places in which to live, work and play are the city's reviving eastern docklands. During the 18th and 19th centuries, a number of warehouses were built on artificial islands in the Entrepot-Haven (Commercial Harbour) area, including KNSM Eiland, Borneo Eiland and Java Eiland. These warehouses are now being turned into a variety of desirable apartments, restaurants and shops. Renovation of the warehouses was begun in the 1990s and is scheduled for completion in 2002.

Above and Opposite
Top: *Amsterdam's street musicians and performers keep visitors and locals entertained year-round.*

Others who helped shape the city include **Hendrik Petrus Berlage** (1856–1934), whose Beurs on the Damrak was regarded as dangerously radical when it was completed in 1903 and is now recognized as a pioneering example of the modern style. **P.L. Kramer** (1881–1961) and **M. de Klerk** (1884–1923), prime exponents of the **Amsterdam School**, used elaborate brickwork to decorate their adventurous buildings, many of them in the Nieuw Zuid (New South) district, which was laid out in the early 19th century.

Literature

If Amsterdam has been pre-eminent in the visual arts for centuries, it has enjoyed a less dazzling reputation in other cultural fields. No Dutch author, poet or playwright enjoys an international reputation comparable to any of the great painters. **Joost van Vondel** (1582–1674), the Dutch poet and dramatist and close contemporary of Rembrandt, is virtually unknown outside his native land.

Classical Music and Opera

The Netherlands has produced no instantly recognized great composer, but its performing musicians are highly regarded worldwide. The city's **Royal Concertgebouw Orchestra** has come a long way since Johannes Brahms, visiting the city for a performance of his work in 1876, described the Dutch as 'wonderful people but dreadful musicians.' The Concertgebouw, built in 1888 by a group of businessmen determined to improve the city's philistine reputation, was restored and extended between 1985 and 1988, giving the orchestra a vastly improved venue. Its acoustics are reputed to be among the finest in the world, and the Royal Concertgebouw Orchestra is claimed to be among the five greatest orchestras in the world.

JOOST VAN VONDEL

Joost van Vondel (1582–1674) was to Dutch poetry and drama what his near contemporary Rembrandt was to painting; indeed, one of the scenes from his towering drama *Gijsbrecht van Amstel* is claimed to have provided the painter with the inspiration for *The Night Watch*. Like Rembrandt, he too went from rags to riches and back again, ending his days on a state pension.

The **Nederlandse Opera** and the **Nationale Ballet** are housed in the **Muziektheater** complex, overlooking the Amstel River. Seating just under 1700 people in its vast auditorium, the theatre – opened amid much controversy in 1986 – gave the two companies a more appropriate home after many years of having to make do with old-fashioned and outmoded venues.

Food and Drink

Dutch cooking is still close to its country roots. Traditional Dutch cooks favour big portions simply cooked and accompanied by plenty of carbohydrates – food created to stick to the ribs of hungry farmers, dockers and fishermen, rather than for the waistline-conscious visitor.

A typical Dutch breakfast comprises bread with jam, honey or other sweet spreads, plenty of cheese, sliced sausage or cold meat (usually ham), and lashings of coffee. Lunch for most Amsterdam workers is a light snack or buffet, not very different from breakfast. The main hot meal of the day in most households is eaten early in the evening and made up of three courses – soup or some other starter, a substantial main course of vegetables, meat and potatoes, often in the form of a stew or casserole, and a sweet dessert. Though many restaurants specializing in Dutch cuisine stay open until later in the

Left: *A range of delicious Dutch cheeses piled high.*

Right: *Amsterdammers will claim that their coffee is the finest in the world.*

evening, reflecting a trend away from early dining, many of the older-fashioned small Dutch restaurants tend to close at 20:00.

Restaurants in Amsterdam offer a host of different eating experiences, from exotic Indonesian, Thai and Chinese to spicy Turkish. Also available are Italian, Greek, Tex-Mex and French. Among the exciting newer trends are the festive Spanish-style tapas restaurants as well as Japanese sushi bars.

Fast food ranges from hamburgers or felafel to shish kebab, pizza and fish and chips. Amsterdam also has its very own home-grown fast food. Pastry shops sell not only delicious sweet pies and pastries but tasty savouries. Butchers' shops frequently sell freshly baked rolls filled with an assortment of cold meats or meat balls, while fishmongers sell bite-sized morsels of fried fish, smoked eel, smoked salmon or shellfish.

But the snack which typifies Amsterdam is **herring**, bought from a fishmonger or from a herring stall. These are dotted all over the city centre, especially in the areas around the market streets. Chopped bits of raw herring are served with chopped onion or pepper and eaten with a cocktail stick.

Vegetarians, vegans and other travellers who require special diets will find that central Amsterdam offers as wide a choice of places to eat as anywhere in Europe. The city's role as a counter-culture capital spawned

---

GENIEVER

Geniever, Amsterdam's traditional spirit, is similar to gin but much more strongly flavoured. It gets its name from *ginebra*, the Spanish word for juniper, which is its main flavouring, but other herbs such as caraway and coriander can also go into the mix. Locals use lots of slang terms for a shot of geniever and the beer chaser which often goes with it. Ask for a *borrel*, a *hassebassie*, *keiltje*, *neutje*, *pikketanussie*, a *recht op en neer* or a *slokkie* – the barman will know what you mean. A beer chaser is a *kopstoot* (knock on the head), a *kabouter pils* (dwarf pils) or *lampie licht* (little lamp), and a large glass of ale a *bakkie* (jar) or a *vaas* (vase).

many 'alternative' eating places, especially in the still faintly bohemian Jordaan area. Though the Jewish community is now only a remnant, the city's Jewish heritage is carried on in a handful of good kosher restaurants, snack bars, bakeries and delicatessen. The presence of substantial Indonesian, Turkish and Middle Eastern communities means there are also numerous eating places catering to Muslim tastes.

Alcohol, coffee and tobacco have important roles to play in the social life of the city. Dutch **coffee**, a taste developed over five centuries, is excellent and is served in bars as well as in cafés. Dutch **beers**, notably Heineken, Amstel and Grolsch, enjoy a worldwide reputation. Beer is served on draught – in small glasses with a disproportionately large head of foam – or in bottles. Amsterdam's native spirit is **geniever**. This highly alcoholic, strongly flavoured beverage is drunk neat and is an acquired taste. Throughout the cosmopolitan city centre, you will find bars serving a wide range of imported beers, wines and spirits as well as local products. The Netherlands is not traditionally a wine-drinking country, and though imported wines are widely available, quality is not always high and prices are much higher than in Europe's wine-producing countries.

> ### BROWN CAFES
>
> Brown cafés – so called because the smoke from centuries of pipes, cigars and cigarettes has kippered walls and ceilings to a rich tan colour – are an Amsterdam institution. Many started life as *proeflokaals* (tasting houses) where potential customers could sample a glass of geniever before buying in quantity. In those days quality control was less thorough than it is now, and each batch of geniever might be different from the last, so customers expected a free sample. These days, you have to pay for your taste in the city's surviving *proeflokalen*.

Below: *Dark and cosy, De Wildeman is a typical 'brown café'.*

2
The Inner City

The **Singel**, the oldest and innermost of Amsterdam's canal rings, forms the southern and western boundary of the inner city, the oldest part of Amsterdam. Singel means 'moat' and in the 15th century this was not only a waterway and drainage channel but an integral part of the city's defences. The very heart of the inner city is the **Old Side**, the oldest continuously inhabited part of the city, bordered by the **Oudezijds Voorburgwal** and **Oudezijds Achterburgwal**. A narrow finger of land, nowhere more than a couple of hundred metres wide and about 1.5km (1 mile) in length, it is also the heart of Amsterdam's **red light district**.

The **Kloveniersburgwal** and **Geldersekade** canals, running between the Amstel and Prins Hendrikkade, are the eastern boundary of the inner city. At the northern end of Geldersekade, where it opens into the harbour, stands the last surviving bastion of Amsterdam's first city wall, named the **Schreierstoren** (Weepers' Tower) because wives and sweethearts gathered here when their menfolk went to sea.

West of the Old Side lies the **New Side** – only relatively new, as it developed in the 15th century – with its western boundary formed by the **Nieuwezijds Voorburgwal**.

CENTRAAL STATION AND DAMRAK
Centraal Station is the gateway to central Amsterdam. Built in 1882–9, at the height of the steam age, it was designed by **P.J.H. Cuypers**, who also designed the

DON'T MISS

*** **Koninklijk Paleis:** the Royal Palace and the city centre's most impressive building.
*** **Amsterdam Historical Museum:** essential viewing for historical context.
*** **Begijnhof:** pretty green courtyard ringed by delightful historic buildings.
*** **Oude Kerk:** the city's oldest church and in sharp contrast to its sleazy red light district surroundings.
** **Nieuwe Kerk:** attractive old church usually with interesting exhibitions.
** **Madame Tussaud's:** the history of the city in wax.

Opposite: *The Oude Kerk at the end of the Damrak.*

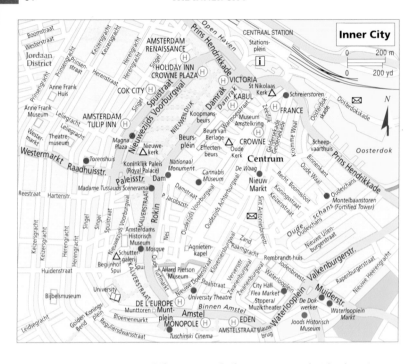

BEURS CLOCKTOWER

The clocktower of the Beurs van Berlage bears the motto *Beidt uw tijd* (Bide your time) – appropriate enough, considering that Berlage was only a runner-up in the first competition to appoint an architect for the building. He won a second contest after the winner of the first was found to have pirated his design from another building.

Rijksmuseum. Built on a man-made island resting on 26,000 wooden piles, the brick towers of its elaborately turretted and ornamented central block shut central Amsterdam off from the open waters of the IJ.

Immediately in front of the station is an area of water called the **Open Haven**, from which canal boats leave on tours of the city. An inner harbour, the **Damrak**, connects with the Open Haven. Damrak is also the name of the street which bisects the city centre from north to south and connects Stationsplein with the Dam, the site of the original settlement on the Amstel.

Midway along the Damrak, **Beursplein** is dominated on its north and east sides by the buildings of the **Beurs van Berlage** and the **Effectenbeurs**. Built in 1903 and named after its architect, Hendrik Petrus Berlage, a pupil of Cuypers, the spare lines and elegant proportions of the Beurs (or Exchange) make it a classic of early 20th-century architecture. Since 1988 the Beurs has been a concert hall and is now the home of Netherlands Philharmonic Orchestra. Its commercial activities have been transferred to the neighbouring Effectenbeurs (Commodities Exchange), on the east side of the square. Next to the simplicity of the Beurs, this neo-Classical building appears a riot of decoration. Its second-floor balcony is supported by four larger-than-life elephant heads and the top floor brickwork is picked out in bright colours. A marble portico surrounds three massive black iron-bound doors.

THE DAM

This is the site of the original settlement which grew up around the castle built by **Gijsbrecht**, first Lord of Amstel, in the 12th century. Under Gijsbrecht and his successors the river was dammed, its waters diverted and the settlement took the name Aemstelle Dam – the dam on the Amstel.

This central square has recently (2000–2001) been smartened up, re-cobbled and pedestrianized but it is still a gathering place for demonstrators aiming to attract attention to a variety of causes, and in summer for street entertainers. It is also a focus for ceremonies surrounding the monarchy. In the middle of the Dam, the 22m (72ft) **Nationaal Monument** (National Monument) commemorates Dutch victims of World War II. Reliefs on the column and its surrounding walls have been sculptured by J.W. Radeler. These reliefs are symbols of war, resistance and peace. The monument was dedicated on 4 May 1956, which was the 11th anniversary of the liberation of the city by Allied troops.

HANDY HOISTS

At first glance, any one of the city's canalside houses can look much like the next. However, the buildings are embellished with elaborate gables and distinctive decorative gablestones. Protruding from many gables is a solid wooden beam, still used to hoist furniture from street- or canal-level through upper storey windows as stairways are far too narrow to accommodate pianos, wardrobes or dining-room tables.

Below: *For almost every visitor, Amsterdam Centraal Station is the real gateway to the city.*

Above: *The Royal Palace is the most imposing historic building in the Netherlands.*

The Dam is an irregular rectangle. From it, a second major traffic artery, the **Rokin**, runs south to the **Muntplein**, where the waters of the Amstel and the Singel meet at the southern tip of the inner city. Overlooking this watery junction is the **Munttoren** (Mint Tower), built in 1622, which stands on the site of the earlier Regulierspoort, the southern gate into the city. The mint of the Dutch Republic was relocated to Amsterdam from Utrecht in 1672, when much of the Netherlands was occupied by the invading French armies of Louis XIV.

PARKING

Cars parked illegally in the city are subject to a fine of Dfl 126,25 and may be wheel-clamped. If the fine is not paid within 24 hours your car will be towed away and it will cost a further Dfl 400 to get it back. Parking in the city costs about Dfl 4,75 per hour. There are illegal deterrents to parking, too. Cars parked on the street are frequently broken into, and it is inadvisable to leave anything of value in your car.

Koninklijk Paleis (Royal Palace) ★★★

The entire west end of the Dam is occupied by the Koninklijk Paleis, built between 1648 and 1655 at the height of the Golden Age. The sober Baroque-Classical façade is crowned by an elaborately carved pediment decorated with unicorns and other allegorical creatures. On the roof stand statues of the Virtues – Peace, Prudence and Justice – while looking down from the back of the building is Atlas, bearing a great green globe and flanked by Temperance and Vigilance. Above all is a huge cupola crowned by a weathervane in the shape of a galleon.

Built as the city's town hall, the palace became a royal residence in 1808, when Louis Bonaparte moved in. On his departure it became the Amsterdam residence of the royal house of Orange, although it remained the property of the city until it was sold to the crown in 1935.

The great halls are lavishly furnished. On the ground floor, biblical allegories in stone decorate the **Marble Tribunal**, once the city's main court-room; condemned prisoners were taken from here to be hanged on a public scaffold on the Dam. Each upper floor room housed a different department of the city administration and is adorned with works of art appropriate to their function.

Most impressive of all is the grand **Burgerzaal** (Citizens' Hall). Louis Bonaparte used it as his throne room: its interior is clad almost entirely in marble and its floor is inlaid with maps of the world. The galleries surrounding the hall and leading to the adjoining rooms are decorated by dynamic canvases of early Dutch history by the masters Govert Flinck, Jacob Jordaens, Jan Lievens and Juriaan Ovens.

Before leaving the palace, visit the 10-minute slide show on historic Amsterdam and check out the relief map of the medieval city on the ground floor. Opening times vary; for more information and guided tours call the Royal Palace (*see* At a Glance, p. 121).

Above: *The dignified Nieuwe Kerk, where kings and queens are crowned.*

Madame Tussaud Scenerama *

Lifelike replicas of celebrities, sporting heroes and historical figures are on display at Dam 7, open daily 10:00–17:30 (July–August 09:30–19:30).

Nieuwe Kerk (New Church) **

New only in relation to the Oude Kerk (*see* p. 43) this church dates from the late 15th century but has been restored after fires. The vaulted interior dates from the 17th century. Kings and queens of the Netherlands are crowned in the church but it is now more an exhibition space than a place of worship, carrying a frequently

> **MISCHIEVOUS CHERUBS**
>
> One of the glories of the Nieuwe Kerk is its 10m (33ft) high pulpit, carved by the sculptor Albert Janszoon Vinckenbrinck over a period of 20 years between 1645 and 1664. The elaborate imagery includes six scenes representing biblical works of mercy, each presented as theatre scenes with three-dimensional wings, which give them remarkable visual depth. Vinckenbrink immortalized himself in his work as the model for the image of St Luke, the patron saint of painters and sculptors. The pulpit has its lighter side too – mischievous cherubs can be seen sliding down the carved wooden handrail.

changing programme of cultural displays. The carved Baroque pulpit and stained glass windows are worth a close look. Open 11:00–17:00 daily.

At Dam 20 stands the Amsterdam version of **Madame Tussaud's** wax museum. Special effects recreate the sounds and sights (though fortunately not the smells) of the city three centuries ago. For contrast, there are also 20th-century displays and an array of effigies of pop stars, politicians and celebrities. The wax museum is open 10:00–17:30 daily from September to June, and 09:30–19:30 daily in July and August.

Nieuwezijds Voorburgwal

Nieuwezijds Voorburgwal, originally the outer limit of the New Side, was a canal and rampart until the building of the Herengracht (*see* p. 71) and the outer canal rings beyond the Singel, when it was filled in to provide a street through the midst of the New Side. It runs parallel to Damrak and Rokin to the west, between the Spui at its southern end, to the Open Haven and Prins Hendrikkade at its northern end. The section south of the Dam and the Royal Palace is the site of a twice-weekly stamp and coin market (open 13:00–16:00 on Wednesday and Saturday).

Below: *The Magna Plaza, a shopper's temple.*

Magna Plaza ★★

This palatial building at Nieuwezijds Voorburgwal 182, with its elaborate bell-tower, turrets, onion-domes and leering gargoyles, is a classic of imitation Dutch Renaissance style. Built in 1908 as the main post office, it looks more like a fairy-tale palace. The stone colonnades

Left: *The Amsterdam Historical Museum houses a fascinating collection.*

and galleries of its interior are richly adorned with shields, crests and gargoyles. It has been converted into an up-market shopping mall.

Amsterdams Historisch Museum ★★★

Housed in one of the city's oldest buildings at Kalverstraat 92, the former Burgerweeshuis (municipal orphanage) was converted into a museum in 1975; the orphanage moved into the buildings of the 15th-century Convent of St Lucy in 1578. The museum is a vivid combination of modern displays and older memorabilia spanning the centuries, intelligently laid out in 20 exhibition rooms. All 20 rooms merit careful inspection, but if time is limited you should certainly not miss the museum's high points. First, climb the giddy spiral stair to the **Bell Room**, where the 17th-century bells from the Munttoren are on display and recorded chimes from the Royal Palace and the city's three great churches can be heard.

The paths taken by Amsterdam's merchant adventurers are shown in lights on a large **map** in another room and are a graphic example of the extent of the city's 16th- and 17th-century trading empire, which by the turn of the 18th century spanned the entire known world and was at the cutting edge of the era of exploration.

CITY SLEIGHS

Horsedrawn traffic was banned from Amsterdam city centre during the 18th century. Instead of coaches, the better-off used wooden sleighs with greased runners which slid easily over the smooth cobbles. The sleighs of wealthy city merchants were as opulently decorated as any wheeled coach. One of them is on display in Room 14 of the Amsterdam Historical Museum.

Even if you do not pause here for refreshment, look into the museum's ground-floor **restaurant**, David and Goliath, for a glimpse of Goliath himself, in the shape of a gigantic armoured statue. Next to him stands a tiny, life-sized David. Between 1650 and 1680 the giant stood in the city's amusement park; his eyes could be made to roll and his head to move – pretty sophisticated stuff for the 17th century.

The **Schuttergalerij** (Guards' Gallery) is a unique covered museum-street lined with group portraits of the militia companies which were first formed in the late 14th century to police and defend the city. Amsterdam's leading painters – among them Rembrandt and Frans Hals – were commissioned to portray the watch companies of their day. The portraits here are by less famous artists. Open 10:00–17:00 Monday–Friday; 11:00–17:00 weekends.

Below: *The 15th-century Begijnhof courtyard seems a world away from the city streets around it.*

Begijnhof ***

At the end of the Schuttergalerij is the Begijnhof, a courtyard of pleasant buildings surrounding a green. Among them, at No. 34, is the oldest house in Amsterdam. This is

the last surviving wooden house in the city, dating from the 15th century. As Amsterdam's population exploded (from 10,000 in 1475 to 100,000 a century later), houses were packed closer and closer together and wooden buildings became an ever greater fire risk. After several devastating conflagrations, the municipality banned all-wood buildings in 1521. Above the door of No. 34 is the legend *Het Wouten Huys*: The Wooden House.

Immediately in front of it is a charming monument to the **Beguines** or Begijns, the 14th-century order of lay sisters who founded their community here in 1346. They rejected the cloistered life of the nunnery – each sister had her own small house and was not subject to the rule of a Mother Superior – but devoted their lives to helping the ill and the poor.

In the centre of the square is the original **Begijnkerk** chapel, built in 1419. The Begijns were deprived of their church during the Reformation in 1578; it stood empty until 1607, when it was taken over by Presbyterian refugees from England, and is still known as the **English Church**. Despite its changes of use, it has the only unaltered medieval church tower in the city. Meanwhile, like other Catholics in the post-Reformation Netherlands, the Begijns had to worship clandestinely; their 'secret' church, next to Het Wouten Huys, is still in use. The last of the Begijns, Sister Antonia, died in 1971, and the pretty little apartments surrounding the square now house elderly widows.

Above: *Elaborately decorated gables surrounding the Begijnhof.*

The Spui

From the south side of the Begijnhof, an arched alleyway leads to the Spui, one of Amsterdam's most pleasant squares. It is a popular meeting place, surrounded by cafés, and the venue for two open air markets. On Fridays (10:00–18:00) the **Spui Boekenmarkt** (Book Market) is crammed with stalls selling antiquarian books and prints. On Sundays (10:00–18:00) the square is taken over by the **Spui Kunstmarkt** (Art Market) with booths selling everything from pretty ceramics to surrealist oils. The quality of the work varies wildly: some of it is exciting and adventurous, some competent but uninspired, and some without discernible merit.

COUGH-INS

During the 1960s the Spui was the meeting place of the Provos, an anarchic hippy movement. They held 'cough-ins' around the Lieverdje statue – given to the city by a major cigarette company – to highlight the dangers of smoking, crammed cigarette vending machines with fake marijuana cigarettes, and – more sensibly – campaigned for free housing for young families, free contraception and abortion clinics, and free "white bicycles" for use by all. The white bicycle plan was actually introduced, but most of the bikes vanished almost overnight, no doubt to be repainted by their new owners.

DIAMONDS

Amsterdam became a centre of the diamond trade in the late 16th century, when its rival Antwerp – at that time Europe's diamond capital – was sacked by the Spanish. Many of the Antwerp traders fled to Amsterdam, taking their skills and trading contacts with them. In the 19th century the diamond trade expanded into a fully industrialized process. Amsterdam remained the diamond capital of the world until World War II, when most of the city's Jewish workers were deported and murdered by the German occupiers. Ironically, post-war Antwerp won back leadership of the world diamond market it lost 350 years earlier.

In the centre of the square stands the figure of a grinning urchin, cap tipped to the back of his head, arms akimbo and socks drooping around his ankles. This is **Het Lieverdje** (The Rascal), the embodiment in bronze of Amsterdam's tradition of irreverent resistance to authority from Philip II of Spain to the present day.

Just across Rokin from the Spui at Oude Turfmarkt 127 is the **Allard Pierson Archaeological Museum**. The museum's extensive collection from the ancient world includes mummies and bronzes from ancient Egypt, Roman statues, and Greek marbles and vases. Open Tuesday–Friday 10:00–17:00; weekends and holidays 13:00–17:00.

THE OLD SIDE AND RED LIGHT DISTRICT

This part of the city presents some of Amsterdam's oddest contrasts. At its upper end are the fleshpots of the city's red light district, known as **De Walletjes**, where the glass windows of the shops display near-naked or provocatively clad women and transvestites who rap on the windows to beckon passers-by. Overlooking them are some of Amsterdam's most prominent churches.

During daylight the sex shops, massage parlours and go-go bars just look sad and seedy; meanwhile, everyday life goes on around them, the ordinary inhabitants of the Old Side apparently oblivious to the ubiquitous sleaze. At night, the glow of coloured neon lends the whole scene a spurious glamour and excitement.

The **Casa Rosso Erotic Theatre** at Oudezijds Voorburgwal 106–108 claims to be 'one of the most superior erotic shows in the world with a tremendous choreography and a touch of class'. It is at least marginally less sleazy than some of the district's smaller and more obvious rip-off joints. Open daily 20:00–02:00; weekends until 03:00.

Near the Casa Rosso at Oudezijds Achterburgwal 54 is the **Erotic Museum**. It advertises five floors of 'erotic enjoyment and

Left: *Relaxing outside one of the city's euphemistically named 'coffee shops'.*
Opposite: *Inner city squats like this are gradually disappearing, but squatters hang on.*

arts' celebrating all that makes De Walletjes notorious, from postcards, books, and videos to an entire floor which has been devoted to sado-masochism. It is open Monday–Thursday and Sunday 11:00–13:00, Friday and Saturday 11:00–14:00.

Oude Kerk (Old Church) ★★★

The Oude Kerk, on the west side of Oudezijds Voorburgwal, overlooks the Old Side and is the oldest church in Amsterdam. Archaeological work indicates a small church existed on this canal-side site as early as the 13th century. The Gothic church tower dates from 1306, but most of the rest of this solid, seemingly massive brick building, dwarfing the houses which surround it, was added or rebuilt in the 16th century. The 65m (210ft) wooden steeple was added in 1566 and the interior has been altered many times over almost seven centuries. The splendid altars of its Roman Catholic era were

---

PORNOGRAPHY

Amsterdam has no inhibitions about what kind of pictorial material may be openly displayed, and some of the video packages, books and even postcards in shop windows are extremely anatomically explicit. If this kind of thing repels you, steer clear of the Nieuwendijk, which has more than its fair share of sleaze, and the Walletjes area, the heart of the red light district.

Above Left: *The dramatic steeple of the Oude Kerk.*
Above Right: *The hidden attic chapel of Ons Lieve Heer op de Solder.*

destroyed during the Reformation, when it became a Protestant place of worship, but three stained glass windows survive from 1555 in the Chapel of Our Lady. They show scenes from the Nativity and Annunciation. Among those buried in the church is Rembrandt's wife, Saskia, whose tomb is on the north side of the church. Open Monday–Saturday 11:00–17:00, Sunday 13:00–17:00.

Museum Amstelkring **

The museum is housed in a 17th-century merchant's home at Oz Voorburgwal 40. Each room is authentically furnished with the parlour in the style of the 18th century to the last detail. At the top of a narrow, ladder-like stair you step into a spacious and richly decorated place of worship. The attic of the house was the last of Amsterdam's *schuilkerks* or clandestine churches, and was known as Ons Lieve Heer op de Solder (Our Dear Lord in the Attic). In post-Reformation Amsterdam Catholic masses were outlawed, but once the first blaze of Protestant fervour faded they were tolerated in private. The church occupies the attic of three adjoining houses

---

CHAPLAIN'S BEDROOM

On your way to the attic church in the Amstelkring Museum look out for the chaplain's tiny bedroom, complete with cupboard-bed, patchwork quilt and chamber pot. On the bedside table are the chaplain's glasses, pipe and cap. The last Catholic chaplain to live here left in 1887 for more spacious quarters, but for two centuries this room was one of the perks of the chaplain's job.

and with two galleries, an organ and religious paintings is far from the cramped refuge its name suggests. Open Monday–Saturday 10:00–17:00; Sunday 13:00–17:00.

Around the Old Side

The University of Amsterdam occupies a number of buildings at the south end of the Old Side. Among them is the **Universiteitsmuseum de Agnietenkapel** (St Agnes Chapel University Museum), dating from 1470. It once housed the Athenaeum Illustre, the academic society out of which the University grew, and now houses a small archive of documents and engravings. Open Monday–Friday 09:00–17:00.

Close by is the **Cannabis Museum**, which traces the positive aspects of marijuana and the cannabis plant through the ages and contrasts its medicinal, environmental and therapeutic benefits with the effects of legal drugs such as tobacco and alcohol. Open daily 10:00–18:00.

Promoting stimulants of a different sort is **Geels & Co. Koffie en Theemuseum** (Coffee and Tea Museum) at Warmoesstraat 67. Geels, one of the city's longest-established importers, sells the best coffee in Amsterdam. A small museum traces the history of coffee and tea from the days of the Dutch East India Company. Open Tuesday and Friday 14:00–16:00, Saturday 14:00–16:30.

Back up on Prins Hendrikkade, near the station, is **St Nicolaas Kerk**. In an overwhelmingly Protestant city, this is one of the few prominent Catholic churches to be found. It was built between 1875 and 1887, much later than the other main churches of the city. However, despite its neo-Renaissance architecture it is a large, clumsy and looming building.

> ### ST NICOLAAS DAY
>
> The otherwise rather dull St Nicolaas Kerk comes into its own on the feast of Saint Nicholas, held on the third Saturday of November with a picturesque festival gathering. Saint Nicholas, the patron saint of merchants and fishermen, naturally has a special place in the hearts of Amsterdammers. He is also the patron saint of children. In Dutch dialect he is called Sinterklaas, but he is more widely known around the world as Santa Claus.

Below: *Sunset over the Open Haven and St Nicolaas Kerk.*

3
The Eastern City

Eastern Amsterdam is bounded by the **River Amstel**, which flows northwards into the city centre to join the Singel, and by the estuary of the River IJ, Amsterdam's highway to the sea. Next to the IJ are the wharfs and man-made islands of the **Oosterdok** (Eastern Docks), linked to the Amstel by a series of canals. The largest of these, Oudeschans, runs through the heart of what was Amsterdam's **Jewish quarter**. Further east is the **Plantage** area, a district of manicured greenery. The Plantage has been a favourite place to escape from the intensely urban inner city for at least three centuries. Most of the east's points of interest lie west of the **Singelgracht**, the longest of the canals linking the Amstel and the docks. Immediately east of this lies the Oosterpark and beyond are residential suburbs.

THE NIEUWMARKT AND THE JEWISH QUARTER
Nieuwmarkt is a wide and somewhat bleak brick-cobbled square enlivened by a row of pleasant cafés and coffee shops, a scattering of snack stalls and the weekly **antique market** (Sunday 09:00–17:00, May–September).

St Antoniesbreestraat runs from the Nieuwmarkt to the St Antoniessluis, where it crosses the Oudeschans canal to meet **Jodenbreestraat**. This street was once the heart of the Jewish quarter but much of its character has been destroyed, first by the Nazi Holocaust and later by the demolition of the entire north side to make way for the dull modern block which occupies the site,

DON'T MISS

*** Rembrandthuis: the artist's former home with a large collection of his drawings and etchings.
*** Jewish Historical Museum: moving memorial to Amsterdam's once numerous Jewish community.
*** Hortus Botanicus Amsterdam: a green escape in a historic garden.
*** Netherlands Maritime Museum: celebrates Amsterdam's seafaring past.
** Waterlooplein market: colourful open-air market.

Opposite: *Oudeschans in the heart of the eastern city.*

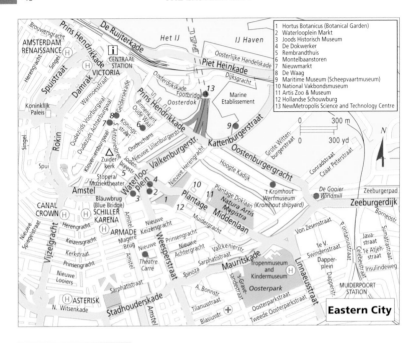

Eastern City

1	Hortus Botanicus (Botanical Garden)
2	Waterlooplein Markt
3	Joods Historisch Museum
4	De Dokwerker
5	Rembrandthuis
6	Montelbaanstoren
7	Nieuwmarkt
8	De Waag
9	Maritime Museum (Scheepvaartmuseum)
10	National Vakbondsmuseum
11	Artis Zoo & Museum
12	Hollandse Schouwburg
13	NewMetropolis Science and Technology Centre

built in 1965. A century ago, the street was a colourful maze of slum apartments and alleys where the poorest Jewish families lived 10 to a room. From 1639 to 1656 it was also the home of Amsterdam's most famous resident, Rembrandt van Rijn.

St Antoniespoort (St Anthony's Gate) ★

The squat, red-brick tower close to the northern corner of the Nieuwmarkt is St Antoniespoort, also known as De Waag (the weigh-gate). Built in 1488, it guarded a gate through the city walls, but a century later Amsterdam had spilled over its old defences and the tower was turned into a weighing place for products from the nearby foundry, which cast cannon and anchors for the ever-expanding Dutch fleet. It was also a courtroom and place of execution. This century it has housed archives, guilds and museums, but at present the building is disused.

Another tower nearby is the **Montelbaanstoren**, overlooking the Oudeschans, a wide waterway lined with houseboats. It was built as a defensive tower in 1512 and prettified a century later by Hendrik de Keyser, who added a steeple topped by an eight-sided upper section. Rembrandt, who lived not far away, made a number of drawings and etchings of the tower.

Zuiderkerk (South Church) ★★★

The Zuiderkerk is a landmark midway along St Antoniesbreestraat. Its graceful spire and clocktower are embellished with red and gold dials. Designed in 1603 by **Hendrik de Keyser**, the Zuiderkerk was the city's first post-Reformation Protestant church and its graceful spire is claimed to have inspired Sir Christopher Wren, architect of St Paul's Cathedral and other historic London churches. Inside is a disappointing permanent exhibition on town planning, but the tower is worth climbing for the views west over the inner city. Open 12:00–17:00 Monday–Friday, and until 20:00 on Thursday; the tower is accessible (from June to September) 14:00–16:00 Wednesday–Saturday.

Het Rembrandthuis ★★★

Rembrandt bought the town house with red shutters at Jodenbreestraat 4–6, close to the St Antonies Sluis, in 1639. He lived here for almost 20 years, until he was declared bankrupt in 1658 and the house was sold. The building is now a museum, with 250 of Rembrandt's etchings on show. All are worth looking at, but there are too many to take in at once. Open Monday–Saturday 10:00–17:00, Sunday 13:00–17:00.

> **REMBRANDT**
>
> Rembrandt van Rijn (1606–69) was born in Leiden, the eighth child of a local miller. He came to Amsterdam while still in his 20s and by 1639, when he bought the house at 4–6 Jodenbreestraat, was already an established painter and married to a wealthy heiress, Saskia van Uylenburgh. The Jewish quarter provided him with many of the models for the biblical themes he loved.

Below: *Rembrandt's former home now houses a crowded collection of his etchings.*

Waterlooplein Market ★★

The daily market held here, though colourful enough, is a mere shadow of the original flea market which developed at the very heart of the Jewish quarter. It sells an intriguing clutter of stalls selling neo-hippy gear, cheap jewellery, junk, old clothes and perhaps even the occasional genuine antique. Open Monday–Friday 09:00–17:00; Saturday 08:30–17:30.

Above: *You never know what might be on sale at Waterlooplein.*
Below: *The restored synagogue now houses the Jewish History Museum.*

The statue of **De Dokwerker** (The Dockworker) in the centre of J.D. Meijerplein, opposite Waterlooplein, was erected in 1952 to honour the dockers who led a general strike in protest against the rounding-up of Jews which began in February 1941. The strike was quickly crushed.

Joods Historisch Museum ★★★

The Jewish Historical Museum is housed in a complex of four former synagogues whose interiors have been painstakingly reconstructed. The oldest, the **Great Synagogue**, built in 1671, was the first synagogue built in western Europe. The opening of the Great Synagogue was followed by the building of the **Obbene Shul** (Upstairs Synagogue) in 1685, the **Dritt Shul** (Third Synagogue) 15 years later and the **Neie Shul** (New Synagogue) in 1752. The collection of religious objects displayed here includes the marvellous marble ark of the Great Synagogue, elaborate silverware, gorgeously embroidered prayer shawls and exhibitions of the work of Dutch Jewish painters.

An exhibition also highlights the the role of Jews in the development of Amsterdam's trade and industry. A grimmer note is struck by the exhibition downstairs, showing false identification papers and ration cards used in the struggle to evade capture by the Nazis. Open 11:00–17:00 daily, except Yom Kippur.

The **Portuguese Synagogue** on Mr Visserplein 3 was built in 1675 and survived the war. It was restored in the 1950s. Its interior, with a lofty, barrel-vaulted roof, was intended by its architect, Elias Bouman, to echo that of the Temple of Solomon as described in the Bible. The huge space is lit by scores of arched windows and original 17th-century brass chandeliers. Open 11:00–17:00 daily, except Jewish holidays.

Muziektheater and Stadhuis complex *

This sprawling complex of modern glass and concrete buildings sited between the Waterlooplein and the River Amstel is familiarly known as the **Stopera**. It houses the National Ballet, the Netherlands Dance Theatre, the Netherlands Opera and the new Stadhuis (Town Hall). Box office open 10:00 until performance Monday–Saturday, 11:30 until performance Sunday.

THE AMSTEL

The River Amstel, flowing northwest into the centre of Amsterdam, curves sharply to the left into the Binnen (Inner) Amstel, a canal basin lined with houseboats which stretches between Waterlooplein and Muntplein, where it meets the Singel. The Amstel separates the eastern part of the city from the southern suburbs and is crossed near its northern end by two attractive bridges.

Crossing the Amstel River at Waterlooplein, where it runs into the Binnen Amstel, the **Blauw Brug** (Blue Bridge) is an imposing 19th-century stone and cast-iron bridge replacing an earlier one traditionally painted in the blue of the Dutch national flag. Built in 1883, it is a copy of Paris's Pont Alexandre. Each of its stone piers is shaped like the prow of a boat, and decorative totem pole-like columns are adorned with yellow crowns, a reminder

Below: *The gold and red crowns on the Blue Bridge were symbols of imperial protection.*

Above: *The Magere Brug is the prettiest of the city's canal bridges.*

LIME TIME

Among the plants cultivated by the Botanical Garden's horticulturalists were limes and other citrus fruit, eventually found to help prevent scurvy, the disease caused by vitamin deficiency which afflicted most long-distance sailors. However, it was the British navy, not the Dutch, which first took to issuing its sailors a daily ration of lime juice – hence the old American nickname for the British, 'lime juicers', later shortened to 'limeys'.

---

of the city's 15th-century imperial status. It is the most elegant of Amsterdam's many bridges, although when it was built more tight-fisted citizens felt its elegance was a scandalous waste of taxpayers' money.

The 80m (250ft) **Magere Brug** (Skinny Bridge) is a copy of an earlier bridge built in 1929, but there has been a bridge here since the 17th century when, according to legend, a footbridge was built for two sisters who lived on this side of the Amstel and wanted easy access to their carriage and horses stabled on the other shore. Their name, it is said, was Magere, which means 'skinny'; but it may just have been called the 'Skinny Bridge' because of its narrow girth. It was widened in 1772, becoming a double drawbridge. The centre section can be raised to allow barges to pass through. Illuminated at night, it is one of Amsterdam's prettiest sights.

Just south of the Magere Brug, on the east bank of the Amstel, is an imposing, domed building. This is the **Theatre Carré**, built in 1887 by the impresario Oscar Carré to house his permanent circus. The circus did not survive its founder and since the beginning of the 20th century it has been a venue for opera and operetta.

THE PLANTAGE
Hortus Botanicus Amsterdam
(Botanical Garden) ***

The Hortus Botanicus was laid out in 1682, when its purpose was primarily scientific and commercial. Here, Amsterdam's doctors and apothecaries grew and studied medicinal herbs, spices and other plants brought back by Dutch explorers from Asia, Africa and the Americas. One of the garden's main sponsors was the Dutch East India Company, which was keen to find new ways of keeping its seamen in good health on long voyages. The horticulturalists also studied new crops and potentially profitable plants – such as coffee, cinnamon, oil palm and pineapple – from Dutch possessions overseas. The first coffee in South America was grown from seeds grown here. These seeds were obtained from plants brought back by Dutch sailors from the East.

The gardens boast more than 2000 kinds of plant, growing in environments which include a medicinal herb garden, an orangery, a monumental palm house and sophisticated tropical greenhouses. In spring there is a superb array of tulips. Open (1 April– 1 October) 09:00–17:00 Monday–Friday, 11:00–17:00 Saturday–Sunday; (rest of year) 09:00–16:00 Monday– Friday, 11:00–16:00 Saturday–Sunday.

Below: *Greenhouses at the Hortus Botanicus shelter plants from every continent.*

PLANTAGE

Amsterdam's explosive growth during its 17th-century Golden Age meant there was no land to spare within the city walls for anything except homes, workshops and warehouses. Even the few courtyards of the city *hofjes* (almshouses) seem like major concessions in what is still one of the most built-up cities in Europe. Amsterdammers in search of a green refuge rented patches of land east of the Amstel, first as vegetable plots, then as more decorative, recreational gardens. Coffee shops and teahouses sprang up to cater to the gardeners and to weekend visitors and the district came to be known as Amsterdam's 'garden of delight'.

AMSTERDAM FOR KIDS

Families with children should plan to visit the Netherlands in summer, when there are plenty of open-air attractions in and around Amsterdam. Many of these are in the eastern part of the city. Try:
• **Hortus Botanicus**, with its huge hothouses full of strange tropical plants;
• **Artis Zoo**, with thousands of birds and animals;
• **Tropenmuseum**, with its fascinating dioramas;
• **Kindermuseum**, dedicated to younger visitors. It has tours on Sundays and public holidays at 12:15, 13:30 and 14:45; reservation is essential, tel: (020) 568-8300.

Nationaal Vakbondsmuseum (Trade Union Museum) ★★★

Found at Henri Polaklaan 9 and known as 'De Burcht van Berlage' (Berlage's Castle), this is one of Amsterdam's most elegant buildings. Commissioned by the General Netherlands Diamond Workers Union and completed in 1900, it was designed by H.P. Berlage. The collection and displays centre on the history of the Dutch trade union movement and the diamond cutting industry. The striking interior, with its splendid staircase, decorative brickwork and soaring arches, grand council room and boardroom with fine murals by the Dutch Impressionist painter Roland Holst, is finely preserved. Open 11:00–17:00 Tuesday–Friday, 13:00–17:00 Saturday and Sunday.

Artis Zoo and Museum ★★

Founded in 1838, Artis is the oldest zoo on the European continent, with 900 animal species and a wealth of plant life. The zoo's paths are dotted with statues, most of them commemorating obscure Dutch botanists and zoologists. Larger animals are in the eastern half of the zoo. A planetarium, geological and zoological museums, an aquarium and a children's playground complement the captive animals. The Zoological Museum which is housed in the aquarium building, has no permanent display but operates a programme of changing exhibitions. Open 09:00–17:00 Monday–Sunday (Museum closed Mondays).

Tropenmuseum (Museum of the Tropics) ★★

Amsterdam's connection with the tropics goes back to the early years of the Dutch East India Company, and you can't help wondering if at least part of their urge was to escape the cold of a Dutch winter.

Exhibits in the museum recreate town and village streets from Asia, Africa, the Arab world, Polynesia and South America, with reconstructed buildings and recorded sounds and sights. Open 10:00–17:00 Monday–Friday, and until 21:30 on Tuesday, 12:00–17:00 Saturday–Sunday.

Below: The gateway to Europe's oldest zoo.

Housed within the Tropenmuseum, the **Kindermuseum** (Children's Museum) is specially targeted at 6 to 12-year olds and has a programme of guided tours and displays on similar themes to the Tropenmuseum.

Above: *The Tropenmuseum preserves the link with the east.*
Below: *Ethnological exhibit at the Tropenmuseum.*

Hollandse Schouwburg ★★

The Hollandse Schouwburg at Plantage Middenlaan 24 was built in 1897 as a venue for light opera, then became the main venue for the early 20th-century revival of Dutch theatre. During World War II, the Nazis used it as a concentration camp assembly point for Dutch Jews, who were sent from here to the transit camp at Westerbork, then to the death camps of Sobibor and Auschwitz.

Since the 1960s the empty, pilastered façade of the theatre has been kept as a ghostly memorial to the victims of the Holocaust. The restored part of the museum includes an exhibition room with videos and documents from the era of Nazi occupation and the deportations. There is a small memorial garden behind the museum. Open 11:00–16:00 Monday–Sunday.

THE EASTERN ISLANDS

The quays of the eastern harbour are lined with tall warehouse buildings. Some of them, like those along **'s-Gravenhekje** and around the **Peperbrug**, date from the 16th and 17th centuries. On the **Entrepotdok**, bonded warehouses on a quayside – once the largest in Europe – have been converted into sought-after apartments.

The eastern islands – **Wittenburg**, **Kattenburg** and **Oostenburg** – protect the inner harbour and are reached by bridges at either end of the Nieuwe Vaart basin. A quayside, called Oostenburgergracht at its eastern end and Kattenburgergracht at its western end, connects the three.

NewMetropolis Science and Technology Centre ★★★

Looking like a grounded spaceship in the middle of the Oosterdok, this new attraction is packed with hands-on experiments in science, engineering and electronics and is ideal for kids of all ages. Situated at 2 Oosterdok, the centre is open 10:00–18:00 Sunday–Thursday, 10:00–21:00 Friday–Saturday.

Werf 't Kromhout
(Kromhout Wharf Museum) *

This dockyard, now an open-air museum, first served the Dutch merchant fleet in the 18th century. By the early 20th century it was building and fitting diesel engines which equipped most of the country's vast fleet of canal barges. Presently under renovation; open Tuesdays only, 10:00–15:00.

On Oostenburgergracht and Cruquiuskade, overlooking the Nieuwe Vaart, is **Molen de Gooier (De Gooier Windmill)**, the last remaining windmill close to the city centre. Built in 1814, it no longer works, but makes a pretty postcard picture.

Netherlands Maritime Museum **

The museum, at Kattenburgerplein 1, has both indoor and outdoor exhibits, including replica 16th- and 17th-century sailing vessels. The main attraction is the square-rigger *Amsterdam*, a replica of an 18th-century Dutch East Indiaman.

In summer, the vessel is crewed by volunteer 'sailors', who attempt to recreate life at sea – swabbing the decks, cooking an authentically unappealing shipboard meal, firing off cannon and conducting a realistic sea-burial, while on the quayside you can watch traditional sailmakers and boatbuilders at work. The museum building dates from 1655 and was originally used by the Dutch admiralty as a warehouse. Open from Tuesday–Sunday 10:00–17:00 mid-June to mid-September. It is also open on Mondays between 10:00–17:00.

WRECKED SHIPS

The original of the East Indiaman recreated for the Maritime Museum, the *Amsterdam*, in fact never saw eastern waters – she sank in the North Sea in 1749 on her maiden voyage. Another unfortunate, and more famous, ship in Dutch history was the *Batavia*, which set out from Amsterdam in October 1628 on one of the first expeditions to Australia. She was wrecked the following year off the Australian coast; her captain made an epic 1900km (1200 mile) journey in an open boat to bring a rescue vessel to the marooned survivors.

Opposite: *Molen de Gooier, Amsterdam's last windmill.*
Below: *The Maritime Museum overlooks the waters of the Oosterdok.*

4
The Museumplein and the Vondelpark

The Museumplein, just south of the Singelgracht which rings inner Amsterdam, is the site of three of the world's finest art collections, and many visitors make an excursion here their top priority. Leading off the Stadhouderskade, the ring road which parallels the Singelgracht, the Museumplein is a busy traffic junction, but the Vondelpark, a few hundred metres away, is the best place in central Amsterdam to escape from the city streets and intensely man-made scenery of the historic city centre for a while and to reflect on the masterpieces displayed in the nearby museums.

The **Rijksmuseum** is one of the greatest museums of art in the world, with an immense collection of superb paintings and other works of art. Only a few hundred metres away, the **Rijksmuseum Vincent van Gogh** has an outstanding collection of the painter's finest work. Slightly less well known, but equally essential viewing, is the **Stedelijk** (Municipal) Museum, with its ever-changing but always challenging selection of work by contemporary artists.

RIJKSMUSEUM ***

The grand brick façade of the Rijksmuseum (National Museum), an unmistakable landmark overlooking the Singelgracht, was designed by **P.J.H. Cuypers**, who also designed Centraal Station. The nucleus of the museum's treasury of art is the royal collection of some 200 paintings amassed by the princes of the House of Orange and

DON'T MISS

*** **Rijksmuseum:** one of the world's finest museums, with an unrivalled collection of Dutch masters.
*** **Rijksmuseum Vincent van Gogh:** the world's greatest collection of Van Gogh's work; also paintings by Gauguin and other contemporary artists.
*** **Stedelijk Museum:** one of the world's top museums of modern art.
** **The Vondelpark:** extensive, lively and laid-back park beyond Museumplein.

Opposite: *The Rijksmuseum's grand façade.*

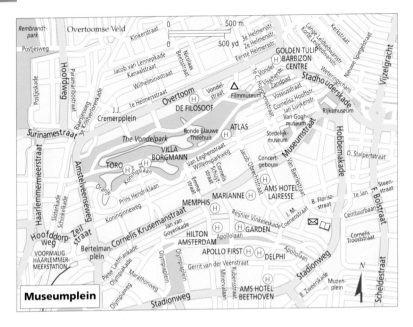

Museumplein

added to as various patriotic patrons of the arts left their collections to the nation. The new museum opened in 1885, and has expanded steadily ever since. It now comprises more than 5000 paintings, a million prints and drawings, and thousands of sculptures. A detailed guide to the museum's displays is available from the information desk in the first-floor foyer.

First Floor

The jewels of the Rijksmuseum collection are on the first floor, where room after room of paintings traces the course of Dutch painting from the stiff religious art of the early medieval era to the increasingly easy and fluid styles of the Renaissance and Golden Age of the 16th and 17th centuries.

Paintings are exhibited more or less in chronological order, putting the works of masters such as **Frans Hals**, **Jacob van Ruisdale** and **Jan Vermeer** into the context of their times. Essential viewing includes the series of panels by the **Master of Alkmaar**, *The Seven Works of Charity*, dating from 1504, in Room 204; two perfect landscapes by **Jan Brueghel the Elder** – neither of them bigger than 15cm by 23cm (6in by 9in) – in Room 207, a tiny circular annex whose walls are covered with delightful miniature portraits and landscapes; and the lively portrait of the cheerfully dishevelled *Merry Drinker* by Frans Hals, whose works dominate Rooms 208–210.

Worth looking out for in Rooms 215 and 216 are the lively portraits by **Jan Steen** of himself and his family, which are full of charm and mark a departure by Dutch painters from their staid tableaux of the wealthy and powerful. Landscapes and townscapes adorn Rooms 217–221, and Room 221A contains four perfect small paintings by Jan Vermeer: *The Milkmaid, The Little Street, Woman Reading a Letter* and *The Love Letter*.

Rembrandt Collection

The superb array of works by Rembrandt is also on this floor. The first of these are encountered in Room 211, where the painter's early work is usually on display with paintings by earlier masters who influenced him, such as **Pieter Lastman**. Neighbouring rooms are filled with the painter's monumental landscapes and detailed representations from Classical and Biblical mythology and landscapes.

> **HIDDEN TALENT**
>
> Along with Rembrandt and Frans Hals, **Jan Vermeer** (1632–75) is regarded as one of the greatest painters of the 17th century, recognized especially for his portrayals of Dutch domesticity. Unlike most of his contemporaries he was far from prolific, producing fewer then 40 paintings in his relatively short life. Rembrandt lived to be 63 and Hals 81; Vermeer died at 42.

Below: *Lively reliefs in the style of the Dutch masters adorn the Rijksmuseum.*

Right: *Tintoretto's beautiful* Otavia Strada, *one of the many fabulous artworks on display at the Rijksmuseum.*
Opposite: *The Rijksmuseum Vincent van Gogh.*

THE NIGHT WATCH

The true name of this most famous of Rembrandt's paintings is in fact *The Guard Company of Captain Frans Banning Cocq and Lieutenant Willem van Ruijtenburch*. Recent restoration revealed that the painting's colours have been darkened by time and dirt and that the 'Night Watch' are actually shown emerging into bright sunlight from the dark shadows of a city gateway.

Portraits of guard companies like these were routinely commissioned by the commanders of Amsterdam's civic militia, but Rembrandt's painting is unusual in its depiction of vigour and action. Paintings of the same subject by other artists, also on display in the museum, show guard companies drawn up stiffly on parade.

Rembrandt's best-known work, usually called *The Night Watch*, is displayed in Room 224. Room 223 houses a display of background material about the picture, including evidence that when painted it was even bigger; some 30cm (12in) were trimmed from the top and 60cm (2ft) from the left hand side in the early 18th century, apparently to make it fit into the space allocated for it in the Stadhuys on the Dam (now the Royal Palace).

Between Room 224 and the foyer is an arcade of rooms called the **Gallery of Honour**, where pride of place is usually given to other Rembrandt masterpieces and works by other painters of the Rembrandt school. Rembrandt's *The Jewish Bride* and *The Syndics*, both painted towards the end of his life, are usually hung in Room 229 and 230. Other painters frequently on display in this gallery include **Ferdinand Bol**, **Govert Flinck** and **Aert de Gelder**, all followers of Rembrandt.

Other Collections

The Rijksmuseum's treasures also include later Dutch painters of the 18th and 19th centuries, exhibited on the ground floor in Rooms 135–137 and 141–149; sculpture and applied art collections in Rooms 238–261 and 162–181; a collection of historical paintings (including dramatic sea battles) in Rooms 101–104; and an Oriental collection on display in the basement. Normally Monday–Sunday 10:00–18:00. From 2001–2003 the Rijksmuseum's galleries are scheduled for renovation, with restricted access, but **The Night Watch** will always be on show. For access details tel: 020 6747000 or check the website: www.rijksmuseum.nl

RIJKSMUSEUM VINCENT VAN GOGH ***

This museum alone provides good enough reason to come to Amsterdam and is one of the city's most popular sights. It boasts the world's biggest and most varied collection of Van Gogh's work, including 200 paintings and 500 drawings. These are complemented by a fine collection of work by Van Gogh's contemporaries, including **Gauguin**, **Monet** and **Toulouse-Lautrec**. Exhibits also include the painter's own collection of engravings and Japanese prints

> ### A LIFE APART
>
> Born in 1853, Vincent van Gogh painted for less than 10 years of his short life. Looking at the glowing works on display in the Rijksmuseum Vincent van Gogh, it is hard to believe that his genius was barely recognized during his short life. He sold only one painting in his lifetime, and lived almost entirely on advances from his younger brother **Theo**, an art dealer, who managed to make a far better living selling paintings than Vincent did painting them. Theo also died young, at the age of 32, and it was Theo's widow **Johanna** who finally brought Vincent's work to a wider audience. Not long after his death, his paintings began to fetch high prices from galleries and collectors worldwide.

Above: *One of the world's leading modern art museums, the Stedelijk Museum.*
Opposite: *The Concertgebouw changed the cultural face of the city.*

TAKING YOUR TIME

Making the most of the Museumplein needs two days – one for the Rijksmuseum, a second for the Vincent van Gogh Museum and the Stedelijk. All three museums have cafeterias, and with a Museumcard you can step outside for a breath of fresh air, then go back to finish your tour. The treasures of Amsterdam's museums are too fabulous to be rushed.

---

and his letters to his brother Theo. The museum, which was completed in 1973, is a spacious, bright building with a rotating exhibition on the ground floor providing an introduction to the painter's life and work.

The main permanent collection of Van Gogh's work hangs on the first floor, with the display constantly changing. In the two years before his death at 37 in 1890, Van Gogh, then living in Arles in the south of France, painted over 200 works, from the muddy fields and leaden clouds of his native Netherlands to the brilliant colours and sunlight of Provence. At one extreme is the earthy *Potato Eaters*, redolent of northern European farm life; at the other the almost hallucinogenic radiance of the sunflowers of southern France. The paintings from this final period of his life are grouped by theme, illustrating how Van Gogh's treatment of the same subject might change almost from day to day, as he discovered, invented and sharpened new techniques. Also on the first floor is the **Print Room**, which gives some clues to Van Gogh's earlier influences, notably the Japanese printmakers Kesai and Hiroshige. In 1999 a dramatic new exhibition wing designed by the Japanese architect Kisho Kurokawa opened. It is used for temporary exhibitions of art and architecture. Open Monday–Sunday 10:00–18:00 .

STEDELIJK MUSEUM ★★★

The solid 19th-century exterior of the Stedelijk Museum (Municipal Museum) belies its adventurous contents. The Stedelijk's innovative temporary exhibitions are always challenging.

The Stedelijk is regarded as one of the world's leading museums of modern art and its permanent collection includes works by **Monet**, **Cezanne** and

Picasso. An imposing marble stair leads to the first floor, where there is a rotating exhibition of works from the permanent collection. These usually include some of the museum's lovely Cezanne landscapes, at least one of the handful of **Van Goghs** left behind when the Van Gogh collection moved to its own museum up the road, and works by **Matisse**, **Chagall** and **Kandinsky**. Pop artists of the 1960s, including **Andy Warhol** and **Roy Lichtenstein**, are well represented, and the museum's fine collection of work by living artists is an eye-opener.

Among the most striking are the unique works by the Russian abstract painter **Kazimir Malevich** and the Dutch painters of **De Stijl** movement, **Piet Mondriaan** and **Theo van Doesberg**. The **Print Room**, downstairs, displays an ever-changing and startlingly eclectic collection of work by living photographers as well as poster and print-makers from earlier decades. Open daily 11:00–17:00 (October–March), 11:00–19:00 (April–September).

Concertgebouw (Concert Hall) ★

At the southern end of Museumplein, the Concert-gebouw is a cultural landmark built in the 1880s by six Amsterdam entrepreneurs in a bid to raise the city's

DE STIJL

The most famous member of the Dutch movement De Stijl (The Style) – whose works dominate the Stedelijk – is undoubtedly **Piet Mondriaan** (1872–1944). Mondriaan spent most of his working life in France and in the USA – he preferred to drop an 'a' and spell his name Mondrian in the French manner, minim-izing his Dutch roots. De Stijl emphasized hard edges, abstract squares and rectan-gles, and bright primary colours, moving as far as possible from any hint of representational art. Other key members included **Theo van Doesberg** (1883–1931), whose works are also exhibit-ed. De Stijl influenced artists worldwide, including the Soviet painter **Kasimir Malevich** (1878–1935); the Stedelijk has a fine col-lection of Malevich's work.

cultural profile. Designed by A.L. van Gendt, the neo-Renaissance building was completed in 1888. Its acoustics – as much by good luck as by good planning – are superb, and it has become a sought-after venue for orchestras and musicians all over the world. Free lunch-time concerts are held on Wednesdays at 12:30.

THE VONDELPARK **

The Vondelpark, a long 48ha (120 acres) rectangle of lawns, trees and lakes slanting southwest from the Singelgracht, was landscaped at the end of the 19th century. The generous sweeps of pathway and wood-land are interspersed with eccentrically shaped stretches of water lined with weeping willows and crossed by toy-like bridges – each a scene from a willow-pattern teacup.

It is a lively place, especially in summer, when it becomes a magnet for sunbathers, kite-fliers, frisbee-players, musicians and street entertainers. In the late 1960s and early 70s it became a mecca for the European counter-culture, with thousands of people camping and creating a summer-long festival atmosphere, but the

Below: *The Vondelpark, a green oasis in the heart of the city.*

hippy dream turned sour with a growth in robberies and hard drug use leading to police cracking down on sleeping in the park.

Popular open-air rock concerts and the impromptu jewellery sellers who flock here on a summer Sunday give the park an agreeably off-beat atmosphere. The park's largest lake, located close to the entrance, is overlooked by the bizarre **Ronde Blauwe Theehuis** (Round Blue Teahouse), a fine specimen of 1930s functionalist architecture. A statue commemorating the poet and playwright Joost van Vondel stands at the entrance to the park.

Landmarks within the park include the **Openlucht Theater** (Open-Air Theatre) where between early June and late August there are open-air performances by all sorts of musicians.

Close to the Vondelpark's Filmmuseum gate is the **Vondelkerk**, another elegant contribution to Amsterdam's architectural heritage by P.J.H. Cuypers, architect of the Rijksmuseum and Centraal Station. Built in the 1870s, it now houses offices.

Nederlands Filmmuseum **

On the outside it's a pretty 19th-century pavilion, very much in tune with its surroundings on the fringe of the Vondelpark. Inside, it is a picture palace from the first golden age of moving pictures. The interior of the Cinema Parisien, Amsterdam's first movie theatre, was salvaged from demolition in 1987 and has been painstakingly restored within the museum. There are three screenings of new and classic films every day as well as an ever-changing programme of interesting exhibitions on the development of the cinema. Open [exhibitions] 12:00–19:00 Monday–Sunday; [film] 19:30–21:30 Monday–Sunday.

> **PIETER CORNELISZ HOOFTSTRAAT**
>
> Running parallel to the northern section of the Vondelpark, this is the city's most luxurious shopping street and is lined with the most expensive designer boutiques. You will see few price labels in these shop windows; this is the part of town where if you have to ask how much it costs, you probably can't afford it.

Below: *Poet and playwright Joost van Vondel is commemorated by a statue.*

5
The Western Canals

Amsterdam's most striking and picturesque buildings and canals are found to the west of the city centre in a rectangle with the Singel as its eastern border, the Singelgracht to the west and the Leidsegracht to the south. Nearest the city centre, and forming a concentric semi-circle round it are the three canals built in the early 17th century to house the city's rapidly growing population – the **Herengracht**, **Keizersgracht** and **Prinsengracht**. Just outside the ring of canals and at the heart of this western area is the **Jordaan**. Originally a district of slums and factories, it is now Amsterdam's prettiest district and the way most visitors imagine Amsterdam, with tall, gabled houses along a tree-lined canal.

BROUWERSGRACHT

The Brouwersgracht (Brewers' Canal) was the heart of 16th- and 17th-century Amsterdam's brewing trade, with hundreds of small breweries supplying homes as well as alehouses. In those days beer was a healthier drink than water and cheaper than tea or coffee, which were both novel and very expensive. By 1500, the city's canals were so filthy that drinking water had to be brought into the city by barge from the relatively clean River Vecht, then distributed by smaller vessels. In winter, rivers might freeze, making drinking water even more expensive and scarce. Today the Brouwersgracht is a quiet backwater lined with trees and tall houses, and only the frequent canal cruise boats disturb its waters.

DON'T MISS

*** **Rommelmarkt:** gloriously eclectic flea-market where you can buy almost anything.
*** **Anne Frank Huis:** always crowded but evocative hiding place of the young Jewish diarist and her family.
** **Theatermuseum:** amusing small museum tracing city's theatrical history.
** **Boerenmarkt:** lively produce and bird market.
** **Westerkerk:** Amsterdam's prettiest church with fine views of the city.

Opposite: *A classic Amsterdam scene along the western canals.*

Western Canals

Antiquemarkt de Looier (Looier Antique Market) ★★

At Elandsgracht 109, this market is a labyrinth of stalls piled high with the clutter of centuries. Some stalls are permanent fixtures, specializing in a favourite genre – antique brassware, say, or glass bottles, or jewellery. Others seem to stock anything that is old. Open 11:00–17:00 Saturday–Wednesday; 11:00–21:00 Thursday.

Woonbootmuseum (Houseboat Museum) ★★

Opposite Prinsengracht 296, located on board the *Hendrika Maria*, this museum gives you a look into life on the water. Open Tuesday–Sunday 10:00–17:00.

Rommelmarkt (Flea Market) ★★★

Close to De Looier market, at Looiersgracht 38, is an even more glorious permanent jumble sale, the Looiersgracht Rommelmarkt. It seems that this is where items end up when they have failed to find a buyer in any of the many other city markets. This market is at its best on Saturday and Sunday, when you never know what you will find. Most weekend visitors to the Rommelmarkt are Amsterdammers in search of bargain clothes, furniture or bric-a-brac, accompanied by a few eagle-eyed antique dealers hunting the stalls for special finds to be sold at a handsome profit. Wednesday is also a jumble day; Monday it becomes a **coin** and **stamp** market, Tuesday is set aside for **books** and **records** and Thursday for used and antique **clothes**. Open 11:00–17:00 Saturday–Thursday.

HERENGRACHT

The Herengracht is the innermost of three concentric canals which ring the city centre from the Brouwersgracht in the northwest to the Amstel in the south. They were built to provide housing land for the city's fast-growing population in the first quarter of the 17th century, when the 12 Year Truce with Spain (1609–21) brought an end to decades of warfare and attracted Protestants fleeing oppression in other lands. The houses of the Herengracht, where the wealthiest gentry and merchants of Amsterdam's Golden Age lived, were among the most magnificent in the city and more than 400 of them have been named national monuments. Sadly, maintaining them is too costly for most people and the majority are now banks and offices. This makes the Herengracht less lively than much of the inner city, with less of the hustle and bustle that so contributes to Amsterdam's charm.

Between the intersection with Raadhuisstraat and the junction with Leidsestraat, Herengracht is a not unattractive jumble of styles and centuries where authentic 17th-century buildings jostle for space with 19th-century revivals and 20th-century imitations.

Above: *Bridges on the Herengracht.*

GABLESTONES

Gablestones, set into walls of old buildings, are protected by law as part of Amsterdam's heritage. When a building is demolished or restored they are salvaged to be mounted in the new façade. These plaques served as address markers before a street numbering system was introduced in the early 19th century. They may show the householder's trade, illustrate the name of a building, or contain a visual pun on the family name. Many people carry on the tradition, especially in the trendy Jordaan neighbourhood where many people have commissioned witty modern stones for their new homes.

MINIATURE THEATRE

One of the highlights of the
Theatre Museum is a miniature theatre commissioned
by **Baron van Slingelandt**,
a Dutch nobleman, in 1781.
A video reveals the ingenious
techniques used to create
spectacular special effects –
such as a storm at sea or
angels descending from the
heavens – which captivated
the Baron's audiences.

Herenmarkt

Close to the junction of Brouwersgracht and Herengracht
is a small square, the Herenmarkt, where the Dutch West
India Company had its headquarters. In the 19th century
the original **West Indisch Huis** (West India House) building was transformed into an orphanage and only the 17th
century courtyard survives from its heyday.

The courtyard is the only part of the building open to
the public and contains a statue of Pieter Stuyvesant,
first governor of the Dutch colony of Nieuw Amsterdam,
now New York.

Theatermuseum ★★

At Herengracht 168, this museum has an eclectic collection of memorabilia ranging from costumes, posters and
an 18th-century miniature theatre to machines used to
produce alarming sound and lighting effects. The
ground floor rooms are decorated with early 18th-century
murals depicting biblical scenes. Open 11:00–17:00
Tuesday–Friday, 13:00–17:00 Saturday and Sunday.

The building next door to the Theatermuseum,
Bartolotti Huis, is also worth a glance. It was designed
in 1615 by Hendrik de Keyser – better known for his
steeples and church-towers – for the wealthy banker
Willem van de Heuvel, and in contrast with the Theatermuseum's neck gable it has an elaborate stepped gable
which owes its present magnificence to a sensitive
restoration in the 1970s.

Below: *The Brouwers-
gracht was once the lively
centre of the Amsterdam
brewing business.*

Bijbels (Bible) Museum ★

Housed in a building at
Herengracht 366, is a collection devoted to retelling
the stories of the Old and
New Testaments. The
models of the Holy Land,
Jerusalem and the Temple
of Solomon are none too
exciting but the plain
elegance of the simple

18th-century wooden interior is almost worth a visit on its own. Open 10:00–17:00 Monday–Saturday; 13:00–17:00 Sunday.

PRINSENGRACHT

This is the outermost of the three canal rings built during Amsterdam's Golden Age to house its newly wealthy merchant aristocracy. On Prinsengracht stand two of the four churches built by the newly triumphant Protestant Reformers of the 17th century, and a fine array of prosperous merchants' mansions of the Golden Age.

Above: *Gable hoists are used to haul furniture up from street level.*

Papeneiland

At the junction of Prinsengracht and Brouwersgracht, this man-made island takes its name, which means 'Papists' Island', from the Carthusian monastery that once stood on this site just outside the medieval city limits. The canal junction here is a tricky one to navigate; if a canal tour boat is passing, pause to admire the skill with which the vessel is piloted through the two narrow bridges which cross the two canals here. The **Papiermolensluis** (Papermill Bridge) across the Brouwersgracht allows barely half a metre's clearance on either side.

Noorderkerk **

The looming bulk of the Noorderkerk (North Church), close to the northern end of the canal, is a prominent landmark. Built in 1620, the church was designed by Hendrik de Keyser, architect of so many of Amsterdam's Golden Age buildings, and Hendrik Jacobszoon Staets. A solid, though well-proportioned building of brown brick and grey slate, it was De Keyser's last project. Its plan is that of a Greek cross, with four arms of equal length radiating from a centre crowned by one of De Keyser's trademark steeples. Open 10:00–16:00 Monday–Saturday.

HENDRIK DE KEYSER

One man more than any other is responsible for shaping central Amsterdam's skyline. Hendrik de Keyser (1565–1621) was the greatest exponent of the Dutch Renaissance style, and his work can be seen all over the city centre.

The city owes three of its most important churches to De Keyser. His first city church, the **Zuiderkerk**, was begun in 1603, and with its elaborate columns is perhaps his most exuberant work.

The **Westerkerk**, begun in 1620 – by which time austere Protestantism had tightened its grip on the city – is plainer but no less elegant, while his last work, the **Noorderkerk**, completed in 1623, is almost grim by comparison.

WAITING FOR A RAINY DAY

At Raadhuistraat 12 is the
Spaarpotten (Moneybox)
Museum, one of the city's
more eccentric little museums,
with a collection of more than
2000 piggy banks and money
boxes on display and 10,000
more in the basement.

On a Saturday from 09:00–17:00 (until 15:00 in winter), the square between the Noorderkerk and the Prinsengracht becomes the **Boerenmarkt**, the place to find cheeses, herbs, honey, freshly baked seed-flavoured bread, or a dozen kinds of wild fungus.

On a Monday (09:00–17:00), the **Noordermarkt**, along the north side of the church, sells old and new clothes, jewellery and bric-a-brac. If you are looking for an antique leather jacket, a beat-up fedora, or something in velvet and old lace, this is the place to come.

Westerkerk (West Church) ★★★

The Westerkerk, with its tower crowned by a blue orb and crown and gilded weathercock, is the prettiest of Amsterdam's four 17th-century churches. It was begun by Hendrik de Keyser in 1619 and completed in 1638, after his death, by his son Pieter and Cornelis Dancker. The neo-Classical interior designed by Jacob van Campen is in the shape of a double cross. The magnificent organ was decorated by Gerard de Lairesse, a pupil of Rembrandt's. It is claimed that Rembrandt is buried here – his tomb is unmarked, but a plaque marks the grave of his son Titus.

Below: *The gold-crowned Westertoren towers over the Prinsengracht.*

The Westertoren (church tower) is Amsterdam's tallest at 85m (251ft). From the top it offers a bird's eye view of the city centre, its ring of canals, and the Jordaan district below. Open 10:00–16:00 Monday–Saturday (April–September), including tower; for reservations, contact the church office (see At a Glance, p. 121).

Anne Frank Huis ★★★

The house at No. 263 was made famous by the diary kept by Anne Frank, who hid with her Jewish family from the Nazis in a secret apartment above her father's herb and spice warehouse. The Franks, the Van Daan family and a dentist named Dussel stayed hidden from July 1942 until

August 1944, when they were betrayed to the Germans. Anne's father was the only one to survive the German concentration camps. The diary was found by an office cleaner and published in 1947.

The crowds of visitors make the visit to the tiny, empty apartment less than moving, but the permanent exhibition that occupies the rest of the building effectively evokes the horror of the Nazi occupation and genocide. Open 09:00–17:00 daily (September–March), 09:00– 21:00 daily (April–August).

Electric Ladyland *

At the corner of Egelantiersgracht and Tweede Leliedwarsstraat, west of Prinsengracht, the world's first museum of fluorescent art in dazzling colours also has amazing displays of fluorescent minerals. It is open Tuesday–Saturday 13:00–18:00.

THE JORDAAN

The Jordaan is bordered by the Prinsengracht, Brouwersgracht, Lijnbaansgracht and Looiersgracht canals. Its higgledy-piggledy houses once lined a watery maze of small canals, most of them – like Lindengracht or Anjeliersgracht – now filled in. These expanded from the original ditches dug to drain the area to provide housing for Amsterdam's fast-expanding population.

Above: *The house at 263 Prinsengracht provided Anne Frank and her family with a secret refuge.*
Below: *Selling flowers in the trendy Jordaan.*

HOFJIES

Amsterdam was among the first cities to develop a municipal social conscience, and from the 17th century provided *hofjes* ('little courtyards' or almshouses) to provide subsidized housing for the elderly and needy. The Karthuizerhof was built in 1650 to provide homes for needy widows and still offers subsidized housing for young people. The architect was Daniel Stalpert. Look out for the two sea monster-shaped handpumps in the courtyard and for the arms of the city – a sailing ship and three St Andrew's crosses – on the inner walls.

The area's name is said to derive from the French *jardin* (garden), a throwback to the Protestant Huguenot refugees who escaped Catholic France to settle here in the 17th century, just when the Jordaan was being built and planted with trees.

The **Bloemgracht,** which cuts across the Jordaan from east to west, was the home of many master craftsmen of various trades. Many of the Bloemgracht's old houses display gablestones which indicate the original owner's trade.

TRIUMPHAL ARCH

The florid triumphal gateway on **Haarlemmerplein**, the busy traffic junction at the northwest corner of the Jordaan, is a poor man's version of the Arc de Triomphe in Paris. It was built for the coronation of King William II in 1840, following the abdication of his father William I (earlier heads of state named William had technically been Stadhouders, appointed by an electoral college, and had not held the royal title). Conspicuous and inelegant, it occupies most of the west side of the square and is a landmark for both the Jordaan and Prinseneiland.

By the 1960s the Jordaan had become the trendy place to be, but there were strong protests against gentrification, which saved it from being completely taken over by upwardly mobile professionals seeking quaint homes to refurbish. The creation of a stock of affordable state housing has ensured the Jordaan has retained some of its down-to-earth character. To see the Jordaan at its bohemian best, try to be here during the 10-day **autumn festival** in September, with drinking, dining, dancing, contests and processions.

Worth looking into are the courtyards of some of the hofjes (almshouses) or the district. The largest of these is the Karthuizershof, Karthuizerstraat 21–131, which still houses young people. The Claes Claesz Hofje at Egelantiersstraat 34–54 was founded in 1626 and houses music students, and the Sint Andrieshofje at Egelantiersgracht 107–114, founded in 1617, is one of the city's oldest.

PRINSENEILAND

For a complete change from the narrow streets and sweeping canals of the Jordaan, head north past **Haarlemmerplein,** a busy traffic junction with a pompous triumphal gateway built for the coronation of King William II in 1840. Across the **Galgenbrug** (Gallows Bridge) is Prinseneiland, an artificial island dredged out of what is now the Westerdok in the 17th century to provide more space for warehouses and merchants' homes, and for their ships to anchor conveniently alongside.

One of the biggest and wealthiest of these warehouses, the **Huys de Drie Prinsen** (House of the Three Princes), was decorated with busts of three Princes of the House of Oranje – William the Silent, Maurice, and Frederick Henry – and gave its name to the island.

Gentrification has transformed Prinseneiland from an out-of-the-way dockland to trendy suburb, and many warehouses have been converted into apartments. Naturally, the most desirable properties are those by the water's edge. The waters of the Westerdok are also a favourite mooring, and several fine old converted sailing barges are permanently moored here.

THE EEL RIOTS

The Lindengracht canal was the scene of one of the Jordaan's many riots when on 25 July 1886 an officious policeman tried to halt a traditional eel-pulling contest (a sort of tug of war using a live eel smeared with soap to make it even more slippery). The crowd objected, the policeman was bundled into a cellar and police reinforcements were showered with flowerpots and roof-tiles. Eventually the army was called in to restore order. In the three-day riot, 26 people were killed and hundreds more injured.

Opposite: *Dark interiors and carpet-covered tables are typical of old-fashioned city taverns.*
Left: *Drawbridge leading onto Prinseneiland.*

6
South of the Centre

South-central Amsterdam is bounded by the Singel and the Amstel in the north and east, the Leidsegracht in the northwest and the Singelgracht on the south and southwest. This slice of the city is even more touristy than the centre, and contains many of Amsterdam's liveliest music and entertainment venues, as well as a number of smaller museums.

REMBRANDTSPLEIN AND SURROUNDS

At its northern end, the Amstel curves sharply westward, turning into the wide basin known as the **Binnen** (Inner) **Amstel**. A popular anchorage for houseboats, it is overlooked by the Stopera complex. The Oudeschans canal runs north to link the Binnen Amstel with the Oosterdok. At its western end, the Binnen Amstel meets the Kloveniersburgwal and the Singel, the original boundaries of medieval Amsterdam.

Close to the south bank of the Binnen Amstel is **Rembrandtsplein**, one of the busiest squares in the city, ringed with cafés and restaurants. In summer, its pavements are packed with café tables; at night, it glows with the garish neon of tacky nightclubs and music bars. Day and night, the Rembrandtsplein's clientele is mostly made up of tourists, and consequently it is not an area of the city that many local people choose to frequent. Rembrandt himself is commemorated by an undistinguished bronze statue in the centre of the square, erected in 1876.

DON'T MISS

*** Six Collection: historic home with a fine collection of works by Rembrandt, Hals and other Dutch masters.
*** Willet Holthuysen Museum: furniture, porcelain, silverware and ornaments collected in a well-preserved 19th-century house.
** Bloemenmarkt: small floating flower market and one of Amsterdam's most-photographed attractions.

Opposite: *Rembrandtsplein is as lively by night as it is by day.*

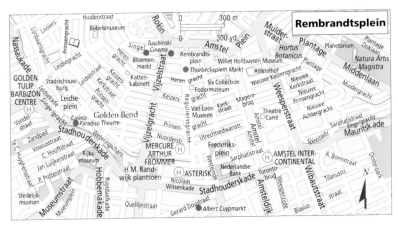

Thorbeckeplein is a small, tree-lined square just off the south side of Rembrandtsplein. It is named after the liberal 19th-century politician Rudolph Thorbecke (1798–1872), whose frock-coated statue stands looking down the Reguliersgracht. The **Thorbeckeplein Art Market** is held around the square on Sundays (March–October, 10:30–18:00). In a similar way to the Spui market, the standard of the works displayed here is a matter of pot luck, but there is always something different to look at.

Midway between Rembrandtsplein and Muntplein, down Reguliersbreestraat, the eccentric **Tuschinski Cinema** stands out from the undistinguished post-war buildings around it. Built in 1921 by Abraham Tuschinksi, its Art Deco exterior of glossy dark brick looks like the castle of some sorceror, while the foyer is a lavish kitsch fantasy of coloured marble, mosaics and brass chandeliers. It still functions as a cinema and is open daily.

Not far from the Rembrandtsplein you can visit the interiors of three of the 17th-century canal houses that abound in the area.

Below: *The 17th-century façade of the Willet Holthuysen Museum.*

Willet Holthuysen Museum ✱✱✱

This beautifully preserved house at Herengracht 605 was built in 1687 for a member of the city council. Inside is a fine collection of ornaments, furniture and porcelain. Most of the exhibits are from the 19th century, when it was the home of Sandra Louise Gertruida Holthuysen and her husband Abraham Willet. The couple left the house and its contents to the city to be dedicated as a museum. They were inveterate collectors of antiques and *objets d'art*, all of which are there to be viewed, along with the gleaming copper and china in the 18th-century basement kitchen.

The rooms are lavishly decorated and the Louis XVI dining room, with its ornate furniture is particularly elegant. Abraham Willet's collection of delicate porcelain from Delft and the Hague is on display in a pretty room overlooking a trim garden lined with topiary. The upper floor bedrooms are now used to display other fine pieces of glass and silverware. Abraham's taste in paintings was less reliable. Most of those on display are mediocre. Open 10:00–17:00 Monday–Friday; 11:00–17:00 Saturday–Sunday.

Six Collection ★★★

Jan Six (1618–1700) was a patron of Rembrandt, and the artist's portrait of him, painted in 1654, is the centrepiece of this collection, housed in the home of the merchant dynasty which Six founded. One of the wealthiest merchant princes of 17th-century Amsterdam, Six became Burgomaster (Mayor) in 1690 at the age of 72. Rembrandt's painting shows him in his prime, relaxed and self-confident. It is among the painter's finest works, with the added bonus that the Six Collection is rarely as crowded as the Rembrandt rooms of the Rijksmuseum. The building dates from 1680, and the collection also includes works by Frans Hals, Jacob van Ruisdael, Pieter Saenredam and a host of other masters. Six family heirlooms on display also include fine china and silverware and furniture as a reminder of the style in which the wealthy families of 17th-century Amsterdam lived. Guided tours take place at 10:00 and 11:00 on Monday, Wednesday and Friday, but only by appointment. To book, contact the Rijksmuseum (*see* At a Glance, p. 121).

ONE MAN, MANY VOTES

Rudolph Thorbecke (1798–1872) whose frock-coated statue stands looking down the Reguliersgracht, headed a committee set up in 1848 by King William II to reform the Dutch parliamentary system. In 1849, with popular revolutions sweeping Europe, rioters in the city demanded equality for all and a series of reforms widening the electoral franchise were pushed through.

Below: *Jan Six, wealthy patron of Rembrandt.*

Van Loon Museum ★★★

Built in 1672, the building at Keizersgracht 672 was in the possession of the Van Loon family for several centuries, and is filled with family heirlooms, furniture and portraits of Van Loon ancestors from the 17th and 18th century. The house is not particularly striking, despite its historic associations (its first owner was **Ferdinand Bol**, a student of Rembrandt's, who lived here until 1680), but the family portraits illustrate the rise of an Amsterdam family from swashbuckling soldiers and privateers of the independence struggle to the dull, prosperous bourgeois who stare from the 19th- and 20th-century paintings and photographs. Open 11:00–17:00 Monday–Tuesday; 13:00–17:00 Sunday.

ALONG THE CANALS

On the Singel, next to the Koningsplein, is the **Bloemenmarkt**, a small floating market comprising a single row of pontoon-booths and one of Amsterdam's most-photographed tourist attractions. On a sunny spring day, the stalls overflowing with potted plants and cut flowers make for a classic Amsterdam postcard shot. The various enclosed booths open onto the street, so their floral glories are hidden until you reach the Bloemenmarkt quay.

The section of the Herengracht between Koningsplein and Vijzelstraat known as the **Golden Bend** was the most sought-after address in 17th-century Amsterdam. At the time, Amsterdam's richest merchants were among the wealthiest men in the world, and they built lavishly by Amsterdam standards. The owners – merchants, bankers, landowners and city burgomasters – could afford twin lots instead of the narrow façades standard everywhere else in the city, and they could afford to build in imported stone, which was used extensively in place of local brick. Costly and exotic materials conveyed wealth in the absence of the elaborate ornamentation favoured by the rich of other contemporary European cities.

GABLE ORNAMENTS

Among Amsterdam's architectural glories are its wealth of ornamented gables, so many of them that counting them all can lead to a stiff neck. Some of the finest are along the Herengracht. Look out for gables richly adorned with fruit and flower carvings, which were popular until the late 18th century, growing ever more elaborate. Earlier houses (from around 1600–65) had simpler step-gables of brick, while elevated step-gables are an intermediate feature. Gables were status symbols: land was always in short supply and the city taxed householders according to the width of their frontage, so houses climbed to giddy heights. Adding another few metres with a high gable was one way to display your wealth.

The houses along this stretch of canal are of greater interest to enthusiasts of Dutch Golden Age architecture, for whom their charm is in their elegant proportions, than to the average sightseer. Among the most attractive is the **De Nuyts** house at Herengracht 575, commissioned in 1668 by the merchant Denys Nuyts and completed in 1672. Many of the exterior details, including the female figures either side of the main window, were added in the 1730s by the then owner, Petronella van Lennep de Neufville, widow of a textile merchant.

On the north bank, at 497 Herengracht, the esoteric **Kattenkabinett** (Cat Museum) will appeal to cat lovers, but it is of little interest to those who are not. It is dedicated to all things feline, and has a changing programme of exhibitions of paintings, pottery, jewellery and portraits of cats and kittens. Open during exhibitions, 11:00–17:00 Tuesday–Saturday, 12:00–17:00 Sunday.

TULIPS

The Dutch obsession with tulips dates from the mid-16th century, when the first bulbs and flowers were brought back from their native Turkey ('tulip' means 'turban' in Turkish). They quickly became an national obsession, and when a Leiden horticulturalist named **Johan van Hoogheland** discovered how to hybridize them to produce different shapes and colours, tulip mania reached new heights. Multi-coloured varieties appeared on the scene; red, pink and white blooms were most highly prized. Bulb-growers set out to produce ever more flamboyant varieties and prices soared. By the mid-1630s speculation in tulip futures was rife, leading eventually to a market crash which left many growers bankrupt before a more realistic attitude asserted itself. Tulips are on sale everywhere in Amsterdam and in particular at the **Bloemenmarkt**. The best place to see tulips outside of Amsterdam is at the **Keukenhof**.

Opposite: *Inside the Van Loon Museum.*
Left: *All the colours of the rainbow can be found at the Bloemenmarkt.*

Spiegelgracht ★★

Almost 100 antique dealers jostle for space along the 300m (1000ft) of this short section of canal which runs between the Herengracht and Singelgracht.

Spiegelgracht began to attract Amsterdam's smarter art and antique dealers around the turn of the century, with the opening of the Rijksmuseum (*see* p. 59), the grand façade of which can be seen at its southern end. The shops and galleries sell everything from affordable curios and collectables to the rarest and costliest of fine furniture, archaeological finds, paintings and sculpture.

A stroll down the Spiegelgracht is an appropriate way to approach Amsterdam's Museumplein, where three museums contain one of the greatest concentrations of magnificent works of art found anywhere in the world. This is perhaps the shortest canal in the city, but metre for metre it is also one of the wealthiest, for it is lined with some of Amsterdam's most expensive and luxurious shops.

Below: *Houseboats on Amsterdam's canals are eagerly sought after.*

HOUSEBOATS

Houseboats are one of the instantly recognized symbols of Amsterdam. About 2400 officially registered houseboats are moored along Amsterdam's canals. In the post-war years, when the city suffered a severe housing shortage, floating homes were a cheap alternative to rented apartments. These days they are eagerly sought after and are no longer cheap. Many are built on the wooden hulls of old Dutch barges, but most are erected on a concrete pontoon. Almost all have piped gas, electricity and all the other modern conveniences.

LEIDSEPLEIN

The Leidseplein, at the corner of the Singelgracht and Leidsegracht, is the liveliest square in Amsterdam, whether on a summer's evening or a winter afternoon. On the square and in the streets around it are more than 100 bars and cafés offering live music for all tastes – in summer almost the entire square is a near-solid mass of café tables, providing an ever-changing cast of street performers with a captive audience. However, the standard of entertainment varies wildly. Adept jugglers and gravity-defying monocyclists alternate with inept mimes and out-of-tune guitarists, but the Leidseplein almost always offers something to keep the visitor amused.

The hulking, overblown **Stadsschouwburg** (City Theatre) at Leidseplein 26 was the home of the National Opera and Netherlands Ballet until their move to the Stopera building on the Binnen Amstel.

The **Melkweg**, a bunker-like brick building on the Lijnbaangracht canal was originally a dairy and is now a time-honoured survivor of the 1960s and early 1970s when Amsterdam established itself as the counter-culture capital of Europe. It was the venue for countless happenings and free concerts and is now an avant-garde venue for all sorts of experimental performance and high-tech art.

Above: *Crammed with café tables, the Leidseplein is the liveliest square in the city.*

A DRY CITY?

After Rembrandt and Van Gogh, canals are Amsterdam's biggest tourist attraction, and tourism is one of the city's major sources of income and employment. The picture every visitor takes home is of waterways lined with picturesque old houses. Yet all this narrowly escaped destruction as recently as the 1960s. In the more prosperous postwar years, the old houses were seen as cramped, chilly and uncomfortable and the canals as an obstacle to motor traffic. City planners seriously considered filling them in and demolishing the old buildings along them. Fortunately for Amsterdam they decided otherwise.

7
The Outer Suburbs

Most visitors to Amsterdam venture beyond the ring of the Singelgracht only to visit the museums or stroll in the Vondelpark. In truth, the outer suburbs are less immediately fascinating than the picturesque inner city, with modern housing, office and shopping developments not so very different from those to be found in any large European city. That said, the outer suburbs – which date mainly from the late 19th and early 20th century – do have some attractions of their own. A ring of **parks** within the perimeter of the A10 motorway which encircles the city provides much-needed green space, the **Amstel River** adds scenic interest, and **ethnic markets**, **shopping streets**, and daring **modern architecture** provide local colour. The district known as the **Nieuw Zuid** (New South) was planned as one of the most daring architectural projects of the 1930s, and many of its innovative buildings still stand.

OUD ZUID (OLD SOUTH)

The Amstel River is the eastern boundary of both the Old and New South districts, which are divided by the Amstel Kanaal. The river is crossed by the unspectacular **Nieuwe Amstelbrug**, east of Sarphatipark, and two large road bridges, the **Berlagebrug** and the **Utrechtsebrug**, connect the New South with the east bank of the Amstel. The **Amsteldijk**, which runs along the river's west bank, is a busy traffic street. For a summer walk along the river, cross to **Weesper Zijde** on the east bank.

DON'T MISS

** Albert Cuypstraat Market:** a sprawling, bustling street market very typical of modern Amsterdam.
** Heineken Brewery Museum:** tours of the historic brewery culminate in free beer tasting.
* **De Pijp:** Interesting inner-city suburb distinguished by pioneering modernist 1920s architecture.
* **Versetzmuseum:** scenes from the German occupation.

Opposite: *Try the tastiest local cheeses at Albert Cuypstraat market.*

The Old South lies between Vondelpark and the
Amstel. Building began in this part of town in the first
half of the 19th century. Near Vondelpark are some of
Amsterdam's most elegant homes and shopping streets,
while the eastern part of the district, separated by the
Boeren-wetering, is dominated by tall tenements, has a
grubbier, livelier character and houses half a dozen different ethnic communities.

Albert Cuypstraat **

Unlike the colourful, bohemian Waterlooplein market,
this is a practical and purposeful place, more dedicated to
inner fortification than outer adornment. As well as
places to buy virtually anything you can eat (and the
natives of Amsterdam will eat virtually anything), there
are stalls selling the peculiar utensils for preparing everything from pickled herring to steamed rice.

This is the widest and busiest shopping street in the
Old South, and its untidy, sprawling street market
(09:30–17:00 Monday–Saturday) spills over into the
surrounding streets for more than 1km (⅔ mile). It is a
noisy, bustling expanse of stalls, shops and ethnic
restaurants (mainly Indonesian and Surinamese) where if
you look hard enough you can buy just about anything.
It's a good place to stock up
on Dutch coffee, cheeses,
chocolates and other
delicacies to take home.

Two streets beyond
Albert Cuypstraat is
Sarphatipark, a tiny patch
of green named after
Samuel Sarphati, the
energetic doctor and do-
gooder who almost single
handedly dragged the city
of Amsterdam out of the
torpor and squalor which
beset it in the early part of
the 19th century.

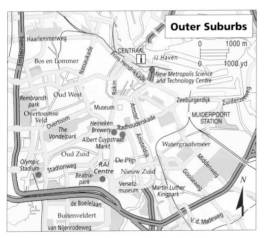

Left: *If you can eat it, you can buy it on the stalls of Albert Cuypstraat.*

De Pijp

South of Sarphatipark, the district known for some long-forgotten reason as De Pijp (the Pipe) is an ethnic patchwork of shops and homes with some notable examples of the adventurous architecture of the pre-war Amsterdam School on its southern fringe.

Among the pioneers of this style of building were Amsterdam's most famous 19th-century architect, **H.P. Berlage** (1856–1934) and his followers **Pieter Kramer** and **Michel de Klerk**, maverick architects who set out to shake Amsterdam's builders from their dull complacency with radical new notions. They designed a number of public buildings and housing projects which can be found in De Pijp and in the neighbouring Nieuw Zuid district. In the Pijp district, the most striking buildings are in the area just north of the Amstel Kanaal, to either side of **Pieter Lodewijk Takstraat**, where between 1918 and 1922 Kramer and de Klerk were commissioned by the Dageraad housing organisation to build an entire neighbourhood. Look out for details such as decorative brickwork and the characteristic sinuous lines of eaves and roof tiles.

KRAMER AND DE KLERK

The pioneering architecture of Kramer and De Klerk was so radically different from what had gone before it that many local people were at first reluctant to live in the apartment blocks they devised for the southern districts.

The architects paid some tribute to tradition by using brick and timber, but also employed new techniques and materials. Brickwork was used to clad reinforced-concrete frames, achieving a mosaic-like effect. Their curving lines, decorative tilework and eccentrically shaped windows and doors are reminiscent of the style of the great Catalan architect Antonio Gaudi, a near-contemporary of the Amsterdam School.

Heineken Brewery Museum ★★

Housed in the former Heineken Brewery at Stadhouderskade 78, built in 1867, the museum is devoted to the beer which famously refreshes the parts other beers cannot reach. Highlights include the stables, which still house heavy dray horses, the vast, gleaming copper brewing vats and, of course, the complimentary glass of beer at the end of the tour. Open for guided tours year-round, Monday–Friday 09:00 and 11:00. Only over 18s are allowed, and no reservations are possible.

CITY SCULPTOR

Sculptor **Hildo Krop** (1884–1970) was the creator of scores of the statues and sculpture which adorn so many of Amsterdam's parks, squares and intersections. For several decades the city's municipal architect, Krop's figures are typically gnarled and dwarf-like. Many of them are to be found in the New South. Along Churchill-laan, which parallels the Amstel Kanaal, miniature reliefs are set into the walls of many buildings, and one of Krop's finest works, *De Geboorte van de Daad* (the Birth of the Deed) can be found on the north side of the canal at Pieter Lodewijk Takstraat.

NIEUW ZUID

South of the Amstel Kanaal many of the public buildings, offices and apartment blocks of the district bear the stamp of the Amsterdam School. The Nieuw Zuid is also home of Amsterdam's main conference and exhibition centre and the **Olympic Stadium**.

RAI Congresgebouw ★★

This conference venue occupies a site on the edge of Nieuw Zuid. It has its own metro light rail station and is the venue, each June, for **Kunst RAI**, an important exhibitions of contemporary art. **Beatrixpark**, next to the RAI centre, borders the Zuider Amstel and Overtoom canals.

Versetzmuseum (Resistance Museum) ★

This museum of World War II Dutch resistance, housed in a former synagogue at Lekstraat 63, has an interesting exhibition of photographs, video and audio tapes. Open Tuesday–Friday 10:00–17:00; weekends 11:00–17:00.

Martin Luther Kingpark *

This park overlooks the Amstel where it curves southwest by Utrechtsebrug. Next to it is **De Mirandabad**, a large complex of indoor and outdoor swimming pools.

AMSTELVEEN

This suburb south of Nieuwe Meer (New Lake) surrounds the Amsterdamse Bos (Amsterdam Forest) planted in the mid-1930s as a job creation project. In the park is the **Nationaal Dachau Monument**, a memorial to those who died at Dachau concentration camp during World War II.

CoBrA

In the centre of Amstelveen, this art museum contains the work of the CoBrA (Copenhagen-Brussels-Amsterdam) school of painters, as well as contemporary artists. Sandergplein 1, Amstelveen open Tuesday–Sunday 11:00–17:00.

OUD WEST

Bordered by the Singelgraght, Kostverlorenvaart and Jacob van Lener canals, the Oud West (Old West) district is a mainly modern residential suburb. On its western edge, the landscaped **Rembrandtpark** is one of the city's largest parks and is favoured by joggers and walkers.

Opposite: *Polished copper brew vats at the Heineken brewery.*
Below: *RAI is a centre for art as well as business.*

8
The Randstad Towns

Within a 60km (37 miles) radius of Amsterdam lie the towns collectively called the Randstad (Round City). An excellent road and rail network means that none of these is more than 45 minutes away from Amsterdam, and many of them repay a half-day or full-day excursion from the city. **The Hague** is the diplomatic and political capital of the Netherlands, with a rich heritage of historic buildings and museums; **Haarlem**, **Utrecht**, **Leiden**, **Delft** and **Gouda** all have picturesque medieval centres; while **Rotterdam**, the Netherlands' biggest city, displays some of the most striking post-war architecture in Europe.

Tourism looms less large in the Randstad towns than the crowded attractions of Amsterdam. While they certainly get their share of visitors (Delft, in particular, can be very busy in spring and summer), most sightseers are there only for a short visit. Not many stay overnight, even in the most popular spots, and outside high season these smaller towns offer a glimpse of everyday Dutch life.

THE HAGUE

Den Haag (The Hague) is the formal capital of the Netherlands and the seat of government (though it is in Amsterdam that the country's monarchs are crowned). It became a royal residence in 1248 when William II, Count of Holland, built a castle here, and in the 16th century it became the capital of the newly independent United Provinces of the Netherlands.

Opposite: *Dutch fields are a sea of colour in spring.*

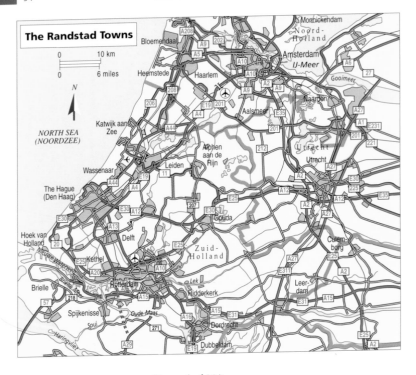

Binnenhof ★★★

The oldest parts of this splendid complex date from the 13th century, when Count Floris V built a castle on the site. In 1585 it became the seat of the States General of the United Provinces. The newer wing, built in 1913, houses the ministry of public affairs and incorporates older elements such as the Louis XIV-style Treveszaal (Hall of Treves) and an octagonal 15th-century turret which is now the Prime Minister's office; he has a fine view looking out over the Hofijver, the decorative lake that runs along the north side of the Binnenhof.

The oldest part of the building is the 13th-century castle. The wooden dome which crowns it is a century-old copy of the original, which was torn down in 1861. Within, the Ridderzaal (Knights' Hall) – a magnificent 38m (118ft) long hall supported by Gothic arches – is used for the ceremonial opening of Parliament performed by the Queen each September. Open 10:00–16:00 Monday–Saturday.

Just to the west of the Binnenhof, in Groenmarkt, is the **Grote Kerk** (St Jacob's Church). Rebuilt after a fire in 1539, the church has been much restored and altered, but is still a treasury of 16th-century craftsmanship. The Renaissance pulpit dates from 1550, the walls bear scutcheons of King Philip the Good, the 14th-century Duke of Burgundy, and his Knights of the Golden Fleece, and two richly stained glass windows are attributed to the mid-16th century artist Dirk Crabeth.

Above: *The Binnenhof, dignified seat of princes and politicians.*

Museums

The Hague's most famous museum is **Mauritshuis (Royal Collection of Paintings)**. A fine example of Dutch Classical Baroque, the building has since 1822 been the home of the Royal Collection of Paintings, one of the finest collections of old Dutch masters, which includes the world's largest collection of Rembrandts and paintings by Frans Hals, Rubens, and Vermeer. Highlights of the Rembrandt collection include four self-portraits which span four decades of the painter's life. Another of the museum's prizes is Paulus Potter's Young Bull, a vast 2.2m by 3.3m (11ft by 7ft) rural scene. Open 10:00–17:00 Tuesday–Saturday; 11:00–17:00 Sunday.

The **Gevangenpoort (Prison Gate) Museum**, is situated in a tower which once guarded the outer portal of the Binnenhof, and from about 1420 the Counts of Holland used it as a jail. It is now a national museum exhibiting grisly instruments of torture. Open Tuesday–Friday 10:00–16:00, Saturday–Sunday 13:00–17:00.

At Lange Vijverberg 14 is **Museum Bredius**, which has a fine collection of works by Rembrandt, Cuyp and Van

---

TOP ATTRACTIONS OF THE HAGUE

*** Mauritshuis (Royal Collection of Paintings): home of the Royal Collection of Paintings, one of the finest collections of old Dutch masters in the world.
*** Panorama Mesdag: amazing panoramic painting of the seaside at Scheveningen, The Hague's beach resort.
** Mesdag Museum: fine collection of 19th-century Dutch and French paintings.
** Madurodam: open air reconstruction of Dutch towns in miniature. Very popular with children.

Above: *Luxury shopping in the Hofweg Passage.*

der Neer in a fine Rococo interior dating from 1756. Open from 12:00–17:00 Tuesday–Sunday.

The **Lange Voorhout Palace Museum** building at Lange Voorhout 74 dates from 1764, when it was the residence of Anthony Patras, the Friesland delegate to the States-General. A royal residence from 1845, it is now a museum with a changing programme of art and historic exhibitions. The interior has some fine Rococo detail, and the façade is a fine example of the transition between Rococo Louis XV and Louis XVI styles. Napoleon spent a night here in 1811. Open 10:00–17:00 Tuesday–Saturday; 11:00–17:00 Sunday.

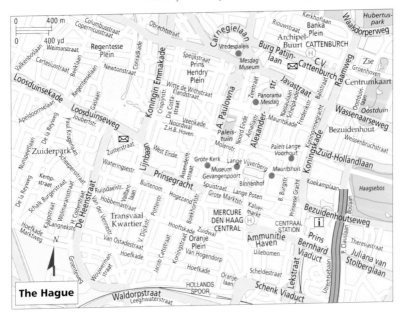

The Hague

Panorama Mesdag ***

The Panorama, painted in 1881 by Hendrik Willem Mesdag (1831–1915), his wife and some friends, is one of the largest paintings in the world. The 15m (45ft) tall canvas is some 112m (400ft) around and is viewed from a low platform. The highly realistic panorama depicts the dunes and beach at Scheveningen, the Hague's seaside suburb. All the scene needs to become a perfect imitation of the real thing is the cry of gulls and a faint smell of fish. It took the painters four months to complete this extraordinary work. Open 10:00–17:00 Monday–Saturday; 12:00–17:00 Sunday.

A few blocks away from the Panorama Mesgad is the **Mesdag Museum**. Mesdag commissioned the building to house his collection of paintings and left it to the Dutch nation on his death. As well as the seascapes favoured by the Dutch painters of the Hague School, it contains paintings by French artists of the Barbizon school, including Millet and Corot. The museum is open 12:00–17:00 Tuesday–Sunday.

> **BY THE SEA**
>
> For a day at the seaside, take tram 1 or 9 from Hague Central Station to **Scheveningen**, the beach resort and fishing town 3km (2 miles) away on the North Sea coast. There is an attractive old harbour, a fine beach (popular and crowded in July and August, too cold for comfort the rest of the year) and a handful of sights including a massive pier and the grandiose Steigenberger Kurhaus Hotel, one of Europe's finest old luxury establishments.

North of the City

The **Omniversum** at Pres. Kennedylaan 5 is a high-tech planetarium-style attraction, operating a changing schedule of pop-science shows with lasers, video and all-around sound hourly on the hour. Hourly programmes 11:00–16:00 Tuesday–Thursday; 11:00–21:00 Friday–Sunday.

Next door is **Haags Gemeentemuseum (Hague Municipal Museum)**. Designed by H.P. Berlage, famed architect of the Amsterdam Stock Exchange and other major buildings in Amsterdam and The Hague, the museum exhibits modern Dutch artists beside earlier 20th-century masters, including Piet Mondriaan, Picasso, Schiele, Monet and Impressionists of the Hague School. Open 11:00–17:00 Tuesday–Sunday.

Below: *The Hague's pedestrian streets are a mix of old and new.*

Madurodam **

This scale-model Dutch town is a combination of 1:25
scale models of buildings and monuments from all over
the Netherlands, complete with tiny toy people, cars,
cows and windmills to lend verisimilitude. The red-tiled
houses come barely to knee height; even the cathedral
bell-tower is only about 5m (16ft) tall. Here a crowd of
tiny tourists are gathered outside a doll's house-sized
model of the Royal Palace; there a Lilliputian sunbather
lies on a roof-top sunbed. After sunset, the miniature
streets are lit by more than 50,000 bulbs. Open daily
09:00–22:30 March–May; 09:00–23:00 June–August; 09:00–
21:30 September; 09:00–18:00 October–early January.

DELFT

Delft is virtually a suburb of The Hague, only 8km (5
miles) distant and five minutes away by train. It is
almost as close to Rotterdam, 11km (7 miles) away.
Among the prettiest small towns in the Netherlands, its
many narrow canals are lined with trees and criss-
crossed by wrought-iron footbridges.
Although Delft has been settled since
the 11th century, most landmarks date
from the 16th century.

Below: *The bridge and gate
to the city of Delft provide a
charming backdrop for this
peaceful canal scene.*

Het Prinsenhof
(Prince's Court) ***

Situated on Sint Agathaplein, this is
Delft's most important historic building.
It was built as the Convent of St Agatha
in the early 15th century and was
William the Silent's headquarters during
his struggle with Spain. William took it
over in 1572 and lived here for 12 years,
until in 1584 he was assassinated by the
fanatic Balthazar Gerard. It is now a
museum devoted to the history of the
Dutch Republic, with a gallery of battle
paintings. In the Moordhal ('Murder
Hall') where William was assassinated

you can see two holes said to have been made by the assassin's bullets. Open 10:00–17:00 Tuesday–Saturday; 13:00– 17:00 Sunday.

Nieuwe Kerk ★★

The 14th-century church on Market Square is the last resting place of William the Silent and of most of his succcsors. William's massive black and white marble sarcophagus is surrounded by marble columns and overlooked by stained glass windows depicting the triumphs of his House. Open 09:00–18:00 Monday–Saturday (April–October), 11:00–16:00 Monday–Friday (November–March).

Museums

The **Museum Lambert van Meerten** is located in a prettily preserved 19th-century house on Oude Delft. It displays a collection of hundreds of 17th- and 18th-century Delft tiles. Open 10:00–17:00 Tuesday–Saturday; 13:00–17:00 Sunday.

Down Koornemarkt is the **Museum Tetar van Elven**. It is named after Paul Tetar van Elven, a 19th-century imitator of Vermeer, who left his gracious 18th-century mansion to the nation with its splendid collection of period furniture, Delftware and paintings. Open 13:00–17:00 Tuesday–Sunday (April–October).

At Korte Geer 1, Delft's 17th-century armoury houses the interesting **Armamentarium** (Delft Military Museum). It contains a very comprehensive exhibition of Dutch military history, weapons, maps and tactics used in the wars against Spain and the Holy Roman Empire. Open 10:00–17:00 Tuesday–Friday; 12:00–17:00 Saturday–Sunday.

Above: *Blue and white chinaware is a favourite souvenir of Delft.*

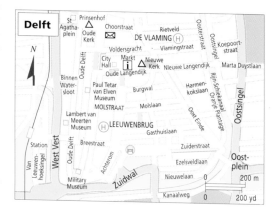

Above: *Containers await shipping at Europort, Rotterdam, the world's busiest port.*

ROTTERDAM

Rotterdam, though an important seaport for more than two centuries, is one of Europe's newest cities. Virtually levelled in bombing by both sides during World War II, Rotterdam has been rebuilt over half a century and boasts an exciting concentration of modern European architecture. As in other Dutch cities, many people still live right in the city centre, humanizing what might otherwise be a visually stunning but sterile environment. Rotterdam is also proud of its collection of public art: monuments, statues and modernistic sculpture adorn its street corners, squares and parks.

The 500m (⅓ mile) wide **River Maas** runs through the city centre and is always busy with shipping heading to and from the 48km (30 mile)s long waterfront of the vast **Europoort** complex downriver. Downtown Rotterdam looks across the **Nieuwe Maas** to **docklands** on the south bank, an area which has become a focus for urban regeneration with the opening in 1996 of the Erasmus suspension bridge linking the two halves of the city.

Prince Hendrik Maritime Museum ★★★

The sea and the city's seafaring connections are well represented in Rotterdam. Chief among the attractions is the maritime museum, rehoused in a striking building at Leuvenhaven 1 in 1986, but dating from 1874. The museum is named after Prins Hendrik (1820–79), nicknamed 'the sailor prince'. The richest exhibits are in the museum's **Treasure House**: trophies and booty brought home by Dutch adventurers of the Golden Age who ranged from the East Indies to the Spanish Main. Moored outside the museum is the restored 19th-century steam cruiser *Buffel*. Open Tuesday–Saturday 10:00–17:00, Sunday 13:00–17:00.

The Leuvenhaven's west quay is a clutter of maritime equipment, forming the collection of the **Open Air Maritime Museum**; tickets are sold in a red lighthouse

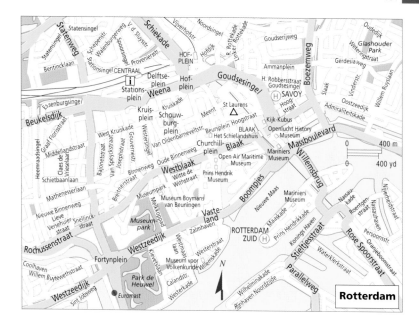

on the pier, which is lined with barges, winches, steam cranes and other maritime paraphernalia. Open 10:00–12:30 and 13:00–16:00 Monday–Friday; 12:00–16:00 Sunday.

Other Maritime Museums

A fleet of traditional Dutch sailing barges berthed opposite Spaanse Kade forms the collection of the **Openlucht Binnenvaart Museum (Open-Air Inland Navigation Museum)**. The Museum also operates the Koningspoort slipway, along the south side of the Spaanse Kade harbour, where you can see these historic vessels being repaired, maintained and restored. Open daily during daylight hours.

The **Mariniers Museum der Koninklijke Marine (Royal Marine Corps Museum)** at Wijnhaven 7–13 is a collection devoted to the Dutch Marine Corps. The newly independent Dutch Republic can take credit for commissioning the first such force of seagoing soldiers: the Royal Marine Corps was founded in 1665. Open 10:00–17:00 Tuesday–Saturday; 11:00–17:00 Sunday.

Above: *Euromast dwarfs every other building in Rotterdam.*

Euromast ★★★

Built in 1960 as a visitor attraction, Euromast is a vertiginous experience. First you take a high-speed lift to the 100m (330ft) high Space Platform. There, sound and lighting effects mimic a real rocket launch and, rotating slowly, you climb into orbit to 185m (610ft). When the nearby medical faculty of the university was completed in 1968 it was 7m (23ft) higher, so Euromast added a second stage to take it to its present height. Open 10:00–19:00 daily (April–September); 10:00–17:00 daily (October–March); in July and August also open Tuesday–Saturday until 22:30.

Rotterdam's Museums

Of the city's museums, the **Museum Boymans-van Beuningen** at Museumpark 18–20 stands out. It houses four excellent collections and among the old masters exhibited are Pieter Brueghel, Hieronymus Bosch and Rembrandt. Da Vinci, Cezanne and Picasso prints and works by Dali, Van Gogh and Appel are also on show. Open 10:00–17:00 Tuesday–Saturday; 11:00–17:00 Sunday.

Also interesting is the **Museum voor Volkenkunde (Museum of Ethnology)** at Willemskade 25. Opened more than a century ago, the museum's collection includes fine art, crafts, religious objects and photographs from all over the world. The emphasis is on former Dutch colonies and the collections are brought to life by a changing programme of slide shows, music, recordings and films. The museum also hosts a varied weekly programme of music, dance, theatre and song. Open 10:00–17:00 Tuesday–Friday; 11:00–17:00 Saturday–Sunday.

An outstandingly pretty Schielandshuis at Korte Hoogstraat 31, a palatial 17th-century mansion with an ornate stucco façade and portico, houses the **Het Schielandshuis (Rotterdam History Museum)**. It contains a collection of art and artefacts celebrating the city from its earliest days. Pride of place is given to the Atlas van Stolk, one of the earliest world atlases which dates from the Golden Age of Dutch overseas expansion and exploration. Open 10:00–17:00 Tuesday–Friday; 11:00–17:00 Saturday–Sunday.

KIJK-KUBUS

The mind-bending cubes of the **Blaak Heights** complex are a dramatic departure from humdrum housing. One of these rather giddy-looking 'pole dwellings' situated at Overblaak 70, was designed by architect **Piet Blom** and completed in 1984. It is open to visitors 11:00–17:00 daily; 11:00–17:00 Friday–Sunday in January–February.

LEIDEN

Leiden is the birthplace of Rembrandt and a historic town in its own right. In 1573–4 it played a heroic role in the wars against Spain, holding out throughout a long siege until liberated by the forces of William of Orange on 3 October 1574, who broke the sea-dykes and sailed to the city's rescue. This event is celebrated to this day in a lively annual festival.

Leiden has one of Europe's oldest and most respected universities and some interesting museums. Buildings surviving from Rembrandt's day include the **Pieterskerk** (St Peter's Church) and the **Stadhuis** (Town Hall) in the town centre.

Rijksmuseum van Oudheden
(National Museum of Antiquities) ★★

The Rijksmuseum van Oudenheden is the finest archaeological museum in the Netherlands, with a collection of mainly Egyptian antiquities. In the lobby looms the reconstructed sanctuary of Isis from the Temple of Taffeh. There are superbly preserved Egyptian, Greek and Roman statues and friezes, mummies and inscriptions.

Above: *Leiden's grand Town Hall dates from Rembrandt's day.*

More interesting to visitors to the Netherlands is the section devoted to local archaeology, recently re-opened and with finds from pre-historic times up to the Middle Ages, including ancient Bronze Age implements and Dark Age Frankish treasures. The 'Archaeology in the Netherlands' collection gives a complete overview of Dutch history, and most of the finds on show have been recovered by the museum's own archaeologists. Open 10:00–17:00 Tuesday–Saturday; 12:00– 17:00 Sunday.

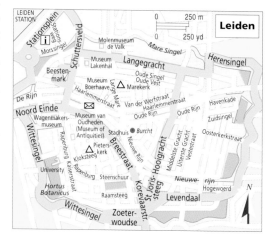

Above: *Molen de Valk, a finely preserved 18th-century mill.*

Stedelijk Museum de Lakenhal ★★★

The Lakenhal on Oude Singel was built in 1640 and became the municipal museum in 1874. Exhibits include paintings by Rembrandt's teachers Swanenburg and Lastman, Jan Lievens, Gerrit Dou, an early work by Rembrandt himself, canvasses by Jan Steen and works by modern artists. Lucas van Leyden's *The Last Judgement* (1572) is one of the gems of the collection. Open 10:00–17:00 Tuesday–Friday; 12:00–17:00 weekends.

Other Museums

These include the **Wagenmakersmuseum** (Cartwrights' Museum) at Oude Varkenmarkt 13, a former workshop which was still making spoked wooden wheels for carts and barrows as recently as 1985; saws and chisels, planes and spokeshaves hang by old workbenches as reminders of vanished skills and there is a small collection of dog-carts, pony-traps and other antique wheeled vehicles. Open 10:00–17:00 Tuesday–Saturday, 12:00–17:00 Sunday.

At Lange St Agnietenstraat 10 is the **Boerhaave Museum**, housed in the former St Cecilia's Hospice and named after Professor Herman Boerhaave, 18th-century botanist, chemist and surgeon. The collection is a hotch potch of antiquated scientific and surgical instruments, including the earliest 18th-century microscopes of Antoni van Leeuwenhoek and the earliest pendulum clocks built by the Dutch physicist Christiaan Huygens.

Also interesting is the spine-chilling reconstruction of an anatomical operating theatre with tiers of wooden seats to allow students a clear view of the dissection taking place on the operating table. Open 10:00–17:00 Tuesday–Saturday; 12:00–17:00 Sunday.

THE SIEGE OF LEIDEN

In April 1574 Leiden was besieged by the Spaniards who defeated all attempts to raise the siege until William the Silent took the desperate measure of breaching the sea-dykes to flood the surrounding countryside and send ships to relieve the city. The day of William's victory, 3 October, is a local holiday. To reward Leiden for its stout resistance, William endowed the town with the first university in the Netherlands. Leiden University is still one of the most respected in Europe.

Molen De Valk (Falcon Windmill) ★★★

A tall, circular brick tower with a gallery just below sail-level, this grain mill on Binnenvestgracht was built in 1743. All seven floors are open, with different displays on each and a fine view from the top three, which hold the milling machinery. The last miller's living quarters on the ground floor have been preserved, with old furniture, paintings and photographs from the beginning of the 20th century. Open 10:00–17:00 Tuesday–Saturday; 13:00–17:00 Sunday.

HAARLEM

Haarlem, capital of the province of North Holland, is just under 20km (16 miles) from Amsterdam. It's a compact city of 150,000 with an attractive medieval city centre. Haarlem is the nexus of the Dutch bulb industry, and in spring is surrounded by fields of brilliantly coloured tulips and daffodils. Like Amsterdam, Haarlem boomed in the 17th century and is built within a concentric system of canal rings. The nearby beach resort of Zandvoort is a popular summer getaway for Amsterdam city-dwellers.

The **Grote Markt**, Haarlem's medieval centrepiece, has changed little since Frans Hals painted it in the 1600s, and is still dominated by impressive medieval buildings.

Sint Bavokerk
(St Bavo's Church) ★★★

The most prominent building on the Grote Markt is the great Gothic church of St Bavo. Built between 1370 and 1520, it is a late Gothic cruciform basilica with a slender wooden tower. Evert Sppowater, master builder of Antwerp, oversaw the addition of the graceful transept between 1445 and 1465 and the Renaissance front chapel on the south side was modernized by De Key in 1593, one of his first commissions as city architect.

> **LOCAL HERO**
>
> One of the best-loved Dutch folk tales is the story of the heroic boy who saved Haarlem from flooding by plugging a hole in the leaking dyke with his finger, loyally staying at his post all night until his cries were heard the following morning. There is nothing traditional about this saccharine story – it was written in 1906 by an American, Mary Mapes Dodge – and you can't help thinking it would have made more sense for its hero, the eight-year-old Peter, to run for help rather than sit there getting wet. However, the municipality of Haarlem in 1950 put up a statue to the little hero at Spaarndam, just outside Haarlem.

Below: *The Sint Bavokerk by night.*

Below: *The Sint Bavokerk
boasts one of the world's
largest organs.*

With its beautiful white arched windows and softly
coloured stonework, the light interior of the church is
one of the prettiest in the Netherlands, dominated by
a splendid **organ**. The entire organ is ornamented in
gilt and crimson and built by the famous Amsterdam
organ-maker Christian Muller in 1738. With 64 regis-
ters and 5000 pipes, it is one of the largest church
organs in the world. Among its admirers
were Handel and the young Wolfgang
Amadeus Mozart, who played here during
his tour of the Low Countries in 1766. Open
08:00–16:00 Monday–Saturday.

Stadhuis (Town Hall) ★★
The oldest parts of the Stadhuis were built
during the 14th century as a hunting lodge
of the Counts of Holland. After the great fire
of 1351, which destroyed a large part of the
city, Count Willem V built the section now
known as the **Count's Hall**, now the city's
gala reception room and open to the public.
Hanging from the ceiling is a gaping whale's
jaw brought back by the Haarlem captain
Jan van Linschoten from his Arctic voyage

of exploration to Novaya Zemlya in 1595. Around the hall are 21 panels portraying the various counts and countesses of Holland in the medieval series called The Dance of Death. Open 08:30–17:00 Monday–Friday.

Also on the Grote Markt and built in 1603, the **Vleeshal** is a fine example of Dutch Renaissance architecture which was originally the city's meat market and its high gables are adorned with the carved heads of sheep and oxen. Opposite is the **Vishal**, built in 1768 to replace the town's 17th-century fish market. Both buildings are now exhibition annexes of the Frans Hals Museum.

Above: *Houses line this attractive canal in Haarlem.*

Frans Hals Museum ★★★

The museum is by no means monopolized by Hals, though it does have more than 20 of his paintings, which are grouped in the Frans Hals Room. The museum's extensive collection of works by other 16th- and 17th-century painters includes masterpieces by Floris van Dijck, Jan Mostaert, Hendrick Cornelisz and Jan van Scorel. An extensive modern collection provides a welcome contrast, and the Restoration Workshop allows visitors to see the painstaking work involved in restoring an old masterpiece to pristine condition. Open 11:00–17:00 Monday–Saturday; 13:00–17:00 Sunday.

On the banks of the Binnen Spaarne the **Teylers Museum**, founded in 1784 by Pieter Teyler van der Hulst, one of Haarlem's wealthier citizens in the late 18th century, is the oldest in the Netherlands. Its collection includes various works by Rembrandt, Raphael and Michaelangelo. Open 10:00–17:00 Tuesday–Saturday; 13:00–17:00 Sunday.

FATHER OF PRINTING

In the middle of Haarlem's Prinsenhof is a statue of **Laurens Coster**, believed (if only by his compatriots) to have invented moveable type. The idea threatened the 15th-century church's monopoly of the printed word, and Coster was accused of sorcery and had to leave town for Germany, where he may have passed on his ideas to **Johannes Gutenberg** (1397–1468), more widely credited as the inventor of printing. A second statue of Coster stands in the Grote Markt.

Above: *Giddy view of Utrecht from the Domtoren.*

UTRECHT

Utrecht was founded in the 8th century, when Benedictine monks under the English Archbishop Willibrod established a foundation to bring Christianity to the regions north of the Rhine. Until supplanted by Amsterdam in the 13th century, it was the most important city in the northern Low Countries.

Domkerk/Domtoren ★★★

At 112m (367ft), the 14th-century Domtoren is the highest church tower in the Netherlands. There are 465 steps leading to the highest gallery, which offers a breathtaking view of the city. The 13-bell carillon has the widest range in Europe; the bells play a different tune at each quarter hour. The topmost tier of the three-tiered tower – built between 1321 and 1382 – is an eight-sided stone lantern.

The opposite side of the Domplein is dominated by the soaring Gothic spires and flying buttresses of the Dom. Begun in 1254, to replace an earlier Romanesque cathedral burned in the great fire of 1253, it was completed in 1520. The nave, built to connect it with the Domtoren, fell in during a great storm in 1674, creating the open space which is now the Domplein. Open 09:00–17:00 daily.

The nearby **Pieterskerk** is an 11th-century Romanesque church, consecrated in 1048, and perhaps the oldest in the Netherlands. Red sandstone pillars support the nave and in the choir are two 12th-century reliefs of Pilate, the Crucifixion and the empty tomb. Bishop Bernold, who commissioned the church and died six years after its completion, was one of a line of Bishops of Utrecht who in the 11th and 12th centuries were the most powerful feudal rulers in the Netherlands. Opening hours vary: enquire at Utrecht VVV.

Centraal Museum ★★★

High points of this collection at Agnietenstraat 1 include a reconstructed Viking ship, dating from around 120AD and a delightful 17th-century doll's house, complete with a family of 23cm (9 in) residents. On the mezzanine floor a room is devoted to the works of **Jan van Scorel**, the painter and inventor from Utrecht sometimes called the 'Dutch Leonardo', and there are works by more modern painters including Van Gogh and Mondriaan. Open 11:00–17:00 Tuesday– Saturday; 12:00–17:00 Sunday.

Other Museums

The **Nederlands Spoorwegmuseum (Netherlands Railway Museum)** is housed in the antique Maliebaan station, and is a rail enthusiast's treasury of more than 60 locomotives, carriages and freight wagons. Models, paintings and films tell the story of railways in the Netherlands. Open 10:00–17:00 Tuesday–Friday; 11:30– 17:00 Saturday–Sunday.

Above: *Beautifully maintained locomotives tell the story of the railways at the Nederlands Spoorwegmuseum.*

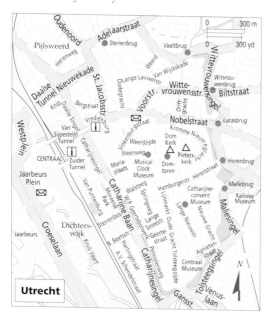

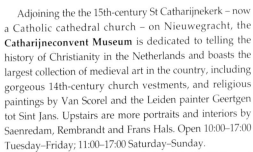

SAY CHEESE

Gouda's **Waag** (Weighhouse) is the symbol of a town associated in so many visitors' minds with fine Dutch cheese. Built by the architect Pieter Post in 1668, it is still the centre of the weekly summer cheese market, when dairy farmers from the surrounding countryside bring their great rounds of yellow cheese to the Markt square to be weighed and sold. Above the entrance a stone relief depicts a pair of giant scales, the emblem of the cheesemakers' guild. If you're there on a Thursday in summer, when the cheeses are being weighed, you will not be allowed to leave without sampling a slice.

Adjoining the the 15th-century St Catharijnekerk – now a Catholic cathedral church – on Nieuwegracht, the **Catharijneconvent Museum** is dedicated to telling the history of Christianity in the Netherlands and boasts the largest collection of medieval art in the country, including gorgeous 14th-century church vestments, and religious paintings by Van Scorel and the Leiden painter Geertgen tot Sint Jans. Upstairs are more portraits and interiors by Saenredam, Rembrandt and Frans Hals. Open 10:00–17:00 Tuesday–Friday; 11:00–17:00 Saturday–Sunday.

Near the Domkerk, on Buurkerkhof, is the **Nationaal Museum 'Van Speelklok tot Pierement'** (Musical Clock and Organ Museum), a collection of automated musical instruments from the 18th century to the present. Open 10:00–17:00 Tuesday–Saturday; 12:00–17:00 Sunday.

GOUDA

Gouda is everybody's idea of a typical Dutch town. A ring of canals surrounds the pretty 15th-century Gothic town centre. Gouda grew up at the junction of the Ijssel and Gouwe rivers and was one of the first Dutch communities to be granted the privileges of a city, with a charter of Count Floris V of Holland from the 13th century.

Grote of St Janskerk (Great or St John's Church) **

The Sint Janskerk on Marktplein, a late Gothic basilica with wooden vaulting, is noted more for its 70 gorgeous stained-glass windows. Of these, some 40 are survivors of the fury of the early Reformation, while the rest are post-reformation additions. They show a variety of scenes from the New and Old Testament and from local history. The window depicting Christ driving the money changers from the temple was the gift of William the Silent, Prince of Orange. Open daily 09:00–17:00 (March–October), 10:00–16:00 (November–February).

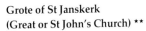

Also on Marktplein is the **Exposeum Goudse Kaaswaag** (Gouda Cheese Museum), housed in the Waag (Weigh-house), which was built in 1668. The museum uses brand new electronics and interactive audio-visual media to tell the visitor all about the age-old craft of cheesemaking. It is open from April–October 13:00–17:00 Tuesday–Sunday.

Facing the Waag across the square is the **Stadhuis** (Town Hall). Built in 1450, it is the oldest free-standing Gothic town hall in the Netherlands, with an ornate façade decorated with antique tapestries. Open Monday–Friday 09:00–17:00.

Above: *Don't leave Gouda without tasting the famous cheese.*
Opposite: *Gouda's Gothic town hall.*

Stedelijk Museum Het Catharina Gasthuis (St Catherine's Hospice Museum) ★★

The museum has an excellent collection, spanning gruesome tools of torture and surgical instruments, 16th-century altarpieces, some fine paintings from the painters of the 19th-century Hague School and the French Barbizon painters, and glittering silver cups and plate which belonged to the medieval guilds. Open 10:00–17:00 Monday–Saturday; 12:00–17:00 Sunday.

Also worth a look is the interesting exhibition at the **Zuidhollands Verzetsmuseum** (South Holland Resistance Museum) at Turfmarkt 30. Open 10:00–17:00 Tuesday–Friday; 12:00–17:00 Saturday–Sunday (April–October).

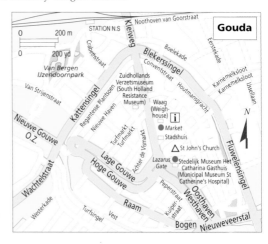

Amsterdam at a Glance

BEST TIMES TO VISIT

Amsterdam is a city to be visited year-round but most people find it at its most pleasant from **April** to **September**. That said, the city is then at its most crowded, accommodation is at a premium, and spring weather is as likely to be cold and wet as it is to be warm and sunny. Amsterdam winters are chilly and damp, but there are no long walks between sights and the cosy cafés and bars seem even more appealing.

GETTING AROUND

Amsterdam is one of Europe's most compact and walkable cities. It takes little more than half an hour to cross the city centre on foot, and many visitors find no need to use the public transport. However, the city has a comprehensive and user-friendly public transport system (GVB) which combines **buses**, **trams**, and a single **Metro** light rail line between Amsterdam Centraal and Amsterdam Amstel main line stations and points south.

INFORMATION AND PASSES
Public transport information, maps and tickets are available from **VVV Amsterdam Tourist Office**, tel: 020 551-2525, e-mail info@amsterdamtourist.nl or from the websites at www.amsterdamtourist.nl or www.visitamsterdam.nl

and from **GVB** offices at Stationsplein, 07:00–19:00 Mon–Fri, 08:00–19:00 weekends; and at Prins Hendrikkade 108–114, 08:30–16:30 Mon–Fri. **Public transport information**, tel: 0900 92 92. The **All Amsterdam Transport Pass** offers unlimited travel by tram, bus, boat and metro and is available at the GVB ticket office at Prins Hendrikkade 108–114 and at Canal Bus moorings at Rijksmuseum, Leidseplein, Centraal Station and Anne Frank House.

TRANSPORT ON CANALS
The **Canal Bus** boat service, tel: 623-9886, operates circular canal routes from Centraal Station with stops at Anne Frank Huis, Keizersgracht/ Raddhuisstraat, Leidseplein, and Rijksmuseum. Canal pedal boats can be rented from **Canal Bike**, 24 Weteringschans, tel: 626-5574, or **Roell Canal Boats**, Mauritskade, tel: 692-9124.

TAXIS
These can be found ranked at Centraal Station but

cannot be flagged down on the street. For **24-hour** taxi service, tel: 677-7777.

MAIN ROUTES
The Inner City
All bus, tram and Metro lines converge on Centraal Station, as do Canal Bus boats.

The East
Metro to Nieuwmarkt, Waterlooplein or Wesperplein; bus 22 to Maritime Museum or Tropenmuseum; tram 9 to 14 to Waterlooplein and Plantage Middenlaan

Museumplein and The Vondelpark
Tram 2 or 5, bus 63; Canal Bus to Rijksmuseum.

The Jordaan
Tram 3 or bus 22 to Haarlemmerplein; tram 13, 14 or 17 to Westerkerk; Canal Bus to Anne Frank Huis.

Leidseplein and Surrounds
Tram routes 1, 2, 5, 6, 7, and 10 converge at Leidseplein.

The South
Metro to Amstel station; tram routes 6, 16 and 24 to

AMSTERDAM	J	F	M	A	M	J	J	A	S	O	N	D
AVERAGE TEMP. °C	4	5	9	14	19	21	22	22	18	13	9	5
AVERAGE TEMP. °F	39	41	48	57	66	70	72	72	64	55	48	41
HOURS OF SUN DAILY	2	2	3	4	4	6	7	7	7	4	3	2
RAINFALL mm	76	50	50	52	55	60	80	80	85	87	90	75
RAINFALL in	3	2	2	2	2.2	2.3	3.2	3.2	3.3	3.4	3.5	3
DAYS OF RAINFALL	20	15	15	15	15	15	15	15	15	20	25	20

Amsterdam at a Glance

Olympisch Stadion; tram routes 12 and 25 to Churchill-laan.

The West

Trams 7, 17, 12, 13 and 14 are the main routes to the western suburbs.

Amsterdam has a very wide choice of places to stay, from five-star international chain hotels to cheap dormitories for budget travellers. However accommodation is comparatively expensive at all levels, with demand matching or exceeding supply almost all year round. The **VVV Tourist Office** at Amsterdam Centraal Station can find accommodation at all price levels.

GRADING

In a **luxury** (four- or five-star) hotel you can expect services and facilities up to the highest international standards. Many of the best city-centre hotels, however, are in historic buildings, and rooms in these can be smaller than in the newer luxury hotels. **Three-star** hotels offer high standards of service, decor and in-room facilities. Most have a breakfast room but few include restaurants and you are unlikely to find facilities such as swimming pools, health centres or business centres. **Two-** and **one-star** hotels

offer simple accommodation, with some *en suite* rooms with shower and WC but no bath, others with shared bathrooms and WCs.

City Centre
LUXURY

Amsterdam Renaissance Hotel, Kattengat 1, tel: (020) 621-2223, fax: (020) 627-5245. In the old city centre, close to Centraal Station and many of the museums; overlooks the canal.

Blakes Hotel Amsterdam, Keizersgracht 384, tel: (020) 530-2010, fax: (020) 530-2030. The city's newest and most luxurious (and expensive) boutique hotel.

Seven One Seven, Prinsengracht 717, tel: (020) 427-0717, fax: (020) 427-0718. New five-star bed and breakfast in total comfort.

Golden Tulip Barbizon Palace, Prins Hendrikkade 59–72, tel: (020) 556-4564, fax: (020) 624-3353. Luxury hotel behind the façades of a row of 17th-century houses, opposite Centraal Station.

Hotel de L'Europe, Nieuwe Doelenstraat 2–8, tel: (020) 531-1777, fax: (020) 531-1778. Amsterdam's most luxurious hotel, built in 1896, renovated in 1993, a model of 19th-century elegance and modern comfort. Overlooks the Amstel, the Munttoren and the Bloemenmarkt.

The Grand, Oudezijds Voorburgwal 197,

tel: (020) 555-3111, fax: (020) 555-3222. Built in 1578 as a royal inn, then used as Amsterdam's city hall, it is a monument in its own right. Very modern within, with facilities including a superb pool and health centre and a stylish canal-front *haute cuisine* restaurant, Café Roux.

Crowne Plaza Amsterdam City Centre, Nieuwezijds Voorburgwal 5, tel: (020) 620-0500, fax: (020) 620-1173. Luxury chain hotel in the heart of the old city.

Golden Tulip Grand Hotel Krasnapolsky, Dam 9, tel: (020) 554-9111, fax: (020) 622-8607. Built in 1866, this five-star hotel opposite the Royal Palace is a favourite Amsterdam rendezvous.

Hotel Pulitzer, Prinsengracht 315-331, tel: (020) 523-5235, fax: (020) 627-6753. The hotel has been created from 24 elegant canalside houses and each of its 231 rooms is decorated with original works of art. Overlooks the Prinsengracht.

Radisson SAS Hotel Amsterdam, Rusland 17, tel: (020) 623-1231, fax: (020) 520-8200. Modern hotel with canal views, built in 1990 within several 19th-century buildings.

American Hotel, Leidsekade 97, tel: (020) 556-3000, fax: (020) 556-3001. One of Amsterdam's most famous luxury hotels, overlooking the Leidseplein.

Amsterdam at a Glance

Swissôtel Amsterdam Ascot, Damrak 96, tel: (020) 522-3000, fax: (020) 522-3223. Built behind a 19th-century façade a comfortable business hotel in the heart of the city.
Canal Crown Hotel, Herengracht 519–525, tel: (020) 420-0055, fax: (020) 420-0993. New small hotel in a historic building on the Herengracht.
Hotel Estherea, Singel 303–309, tel: (020) 624-5146, fax: (020) 623-9001. Comfortable, family-owned four-star hotel housed in 17th-century buildings.
Jolly Hotel Carlton, Vijzelstraat 4, tel: (020) 622-2266, fax: (020) 626-6183. Next to the Amstel, Munttoren and the Bloemenmarkt, four-star hotel belonging to an Italian chain.
Die Port van Cleve, Nieuwezijds Voorburgwal 176–180, tel: (020) 624-4860, fax: (020) 622-0240. Comfortable four-star hotel which houses 'De Poort', Amsterdam's most famous historic restaurant.
Victoria Hotel Amsterdam, Damrak 1–5, tel: (020) 623-4255, fax: (020) 625-2997. Central four-star hotel opposite Centraal Station.

MID-RANGE
Ambassade Hotel, Herengracht 335–353, tel: (020) 626-2333, fax: (020) 624-5321. Comfortable hotel

with lots of character and a central location on the Herengracht. Excellent value.
Canal House Hotel, Keizersgracht 148, tel: (020) 622-5182, fax: (020) 624-1317. Elegant, small three-star hotel in a 17th-century building. Rooms furnished with antiques.
Cok City Hotel, Nieuwezijds Voorburgwal 50, tel: (020) 422-0011, fax: (020) 420-0357. Conveniently located three-star hotel.
Eden Hotel Amsterdam, Amstel 144, tel: (020) 530-7878, fax: (020) 624-2946. Comfortable, well located three-star between the Amstel and Rembrandtplein.
Mercure Arthur Frommer, Noorderstraat 46, tel: (020) 622-0328, fax: (020) 622-3208. Part of the three-star French chain, close to the Noorderkerk and named after the doyen of budget travel guidebook writers.

BUDGET
Bodeman, Rokin 154–156, tel: (020) 620-1558, fax: (020) 624-9995.
Rokin, Rokin 73, tel: (020) 626-7485, fax: (020) 625-6453. The hotels Bodeman and Rokin are two-stars, located near the Dam and the Royal Palace.
City Hotel Amsterdam, Prins Hendrikkade 130, tel: (020) 623-0836, fax: (020) 638-3799. Two-star, close to Centraal Station.

Multatuli, Prins Hendrikkade 12, tel: (020) 627-4282, fax: (020) 620-8003. Good-value two-star near station, clean and bright.
Imperial, Thorbeckeplein 9, tel: (020) 622-0051, fax: (020) 624-5836. Pleasantly located two-star close to museums.
De Korenaer, Damrak 50, tel: (020) 622-0855, fax: (020) 620-7685. Very central two-star opposite station.
Hotel Schirmann, Prins Hendrikkade 23, tel: (020) 624-1942, fax: (020) 622-7759. Labyrinthine one-star hotel, with tiny rooms but handy for station and coffee shops.

Outside the Centre
LUXURY
Amstel Inter-Continental Amsterdam, Prof. Tulpplein 1, tel: (020) 622-6060, fax: (020) 622-5808. Historic hotel opened in 1667 and renovated in 1992. Elegant building overlooking the River Amstel.
Le Meridien Apollo, Apollolaan 2, tel: (020) 673-5922, fax: (020) 570-5744. Business hotel close to Museumplein and convenient for RAI conference centre and World Trade Centre.
Bilderberg Garden Hotel, Dijsselhofplantsoen 7, tel: (020) 664-2220, fax: (020) 679-9356. Bright, modern hotel, smaller than most in five-star bracket with 98

Amsterdam at a Glance

rooms and a *haute cuisine* French restaurant, the Mangerie de Kersentuin.

Amsterdam Hilton, Apollolaan 138–140, tel: (020) 710-6000, fax: (020) 710-9000. Canalside luxury hotel with its own marina and fleet of boats for hire.

Holiday Inn Amsterdam, De Boelelaan 2, tel: (020) 646-2300, fax: (020) 646-4790. De luxe international chain museum situated opposite the Amstelpark and only 500m away from the RAI exhibition and congress centre.

Amsterdam Marriott Hotel, Stadhouderskade 12, tel: (020) 607-5555, fax: (020) 607-5511. Next to Vondelpark and Leidseplein. Handy for museums and city centre.

Hotel Okura Amsterdam, Ferdinand Bolstraat 333, tel: (020) 678-7111, fax: (020) 671-2344. Functional but convenient five-star, five minutes walk from the RAI centre. Facilities include four restaurants, two of them Japanese.

Hotel Apollofirst, Apollolaan 123, tel: (020) 673-0333, fax: (020) 675-0348. Elegant small family-owned hotel.

Parkhotel, Stadhouderskade 25, tel: (020) 671-1222, fax: (020) 664-9455. Comfortable four-star, around the corner from the Van Gogh Museum and Rijksmuseum.

MID-RANGE

Toro Hotel, Koningslaan 64, 1075 AG Amsterdam, tel: (020) 673-7223, tel: (020) 675-0031. Housed in two pretty turn-of-the-century homes, this small 22-room hotel is decorated with antiques and located on the edge of the Vondelpark, overlooking the lake.

Schiphol Airport

All airport hotels provide free shuttle bus service to and from the airport terminal. There is no budget accommodation at the airport.

LUXURY

Golden Tulip Hotel Barbizon Schiphol, Kruisweg 495, tel: (020) 655-0500, fax: (020) 653-4999. Luxury hotel situated close to the airport terminal.

Amsterdam Schiphol Airport Hilton, Herbergierstraat 1, tel: (020) 603-4567, fax: (020) 603-4781. In the airport complex, two minutes from terminal by shuttle.

Holiday Inn Crowne Plaza Amsterdam-Schiphol, Planeetbaan 2, Hoofddorp, tel: (023) 565-0000, fax: (023) 565-0521. Luxury hotel 2km (1¼ miles) from airport.

MID-RANGE

Hotel Mercure Schiphol Terminal, tel: (020) 604-1339, fax: (020) 615-9027. The only hotel actually in the terminal, accessible from the arrivals level in the south

lounge and the upper floor west lounge.

Dorint Hotel Schiphol Amsterdam, Sloterweg 299, tel: (020) 658-8288, fax: (020) 659-7101. Four-star hotel midway between the airport and central Amsterdam. Free shuttle bus to terminal every 20 minutes.

Campsites

Camping Vliegenbos, Meeuwenlaan 138, tel: (020) 636-8855, fax: (020) 632-2723. Across the IJ in north Amsterdam, 10 minutes from the centre by ferry, this well-appointed campsite has its own shop and restaurant, washing machines and driers, and accommodation in hiker's cabins for those without tents. Open 1 April–30 September.

Amsterdam has a tremen-

WHERE TO EAT

dous choice of places to eat, most of them concentrated in the city centre. Every cuisine in the world is represented. Restaurants found around the **Leidseplein** and **Rembrandtplein** areas tend to be very touristy, with prices and menus to match. Cheaper places to eat, many of them offering Middle Eastern, Greek, Indonesian or Turkish menus, can be found around the **Nieuwendijk** and **Zeedijk** near Centraal Station. A number of small, pleasant restaurants with an

Amsterdam at a Glance

affordable menu and a faintly bohemian air are scattered around the **Jordaan** district. For those on a tight budget, there are also plenty of snack bars selling burgers, kebabs, chips, felafel and other cheap and filling snacks on these streets. Many of the city's finest restaurants are in its top city-centre hotels.

City Centre

LUXURY

De Poort, Hotel die Port van Cleve (see Where to Stay). Fine old Dutch restaurant, noted for its steaks.

Café Roux, Grand Hotel (see Where to Stay). Excellent Roux Brothers restaurant, open lunch and dinner.

De Goudsbloem, Pulitzer Hotel (see Where to Stay). Fine small hotel restaurant; with emphasis on French cooking and Amsterdam's longest wine list.

Christophe, Leliegracht 46, tel: (020) 625-0807. French restaurant with one Michelin star, probably the best in Amsterdam. Dinner only, booking essential.

De Trechter, Hobbemakade 63, tel: (020) 671-1263. French restaurant with one Michelin star. Dinner only.

't Swarte Schaep, Korte Leidsedwarsstraat 24, tel: (020) 622-3021. Just off the Leidseplein. Hearty Dutch meals served; go for the 17th-century interior as much as for the food.

D'Vijff Vlieghen, Spuistraat 294, tel: (020) 624-8369. The most famous and the best of Amsterdam's Dutch restaurants. Lots of tiny rooms in 17th-century building.

De Oesterbar, Leidseplein 10, tel: (020) 623-2988. Upmarket seafood restaurant.

Les Quatre Canetons, Prinsengracht 1111, tel: (020) 624-6307. Good quality French restaurant.

MID-RANGE

New Bali, Leidsestraat 95, tel: (020) 622-7878, fax: (020) 626-2465. Amsterdam's best Indonesian restaurant. The huge *rijstaffel* of 20 different dishes is real value for money.

't Haringhuis, Oude Doelenstraat 18, tel: (020) 622-1284. The best place in town to try Dutch herring and other tasy seafood dishes.

Tapasbar A la Plancha, 1e Looierdwarsstraat 15, tel: (020) 420-3633. Cheerful, affordable Spanish restaurant offering tapas dishes and wines by the glass.

Zushi, Amstel 20, tel: (020) 330-6882. One of the new trendy sushi bars with automat price-coded service.

In de Waag, Nieuwmarkt 4, tel: (020) 422-7772. International cuisine in café-restaurant located inside the old 15th-century city gate.

Sea Palace, Oosterdokskade 8, tel: (020) 626-4777. Near Centraal Station, this vast, Hong Kong-style floating

restaurant has a fine view of the Oosterdok and the IJ.

Haesje Claes, Spuistraat 273, tel: (020) 624-9998. Affordable restaurant, specializing in Dutch regional dishes.

BUDGET

Soup en zo, Jodenbreestraat 94a, tel: (020) 422-2243. Soup and snack restaurant which also serves freshly squeezed juices.

Sap & Soup, Haarlemmerstraat 68, tel: (020) 320-9190. The name means 'juice and soup' and that is what this outfit serves.

Turkiye, Nieuwezijds Voorburgwal 169, tel: (020) 622-9919. Good value-for-money Turkish restaurant.

Sal Meijer Sandwichshop, Scheldestraat 45, tel: (020) 673-1313. Kosher sandwiches to eat in or take away.

Eten and Drinken, Warmoesstraat 7 (no phone) is the best bargain in town, open almost around the clock, with a dish of the day served with generous helpings of fries and salad.

Oibibio, Prins Hendrikkade 20–21, tel: (020) 553-9355. Bright, cheerful, affordable vegetarian café-restaurant.

TRADITIONAL TAVERNS

Café Chris, Bloemstraat 42, tel: (020) 624-5942. Old tavern dating from 1624. Builders working on the nearby Westerkerk are said to have received their wages here.

Amsterdam at a Glance

Café Karpershoek, Martelaarsgracht 2, tel: 624-7886. Opened in 1629 and still more popular with locals than visitors. Sit outside for a view of the station and the Open Haven. Opens at 07:00, so a good place for an early morning coffee if you have an early train to catch.

Café de Druif, Rapenburg 83, tel: (020) 624-4530. Claimed to have been here since 1631 and to have been a favourite drinking place of the legendary naval hero Piet Heyn; however, as Heyn died in 1629, this tradition does not bear close examination.

Café Papeneiland, Prinsengracht 2, tel: (020) 624-1989. Opened in 1642 on the edge of the Jordaan, beside the Brouwersgracht. The exterior has beautiful step gables.

De Drie Fleschjes, Gravenstraat 18, tel: (020) 624-8443. Opened in 1650, this café has been the tasting-house for Hendrik Bootz liqueurs since 1816.

Café Hoppe, Spui 18–20, tel: (020) 624-7849. A very popular old café in the heart of the city, whose clientele often spills out onto the street outside during summer.

Café Kalkhoven, Prinsengracht 283, tel: (020) 624-9649. Facing the Westerkerk, this café may have been open as long ago as 1630, making it the fourth oldest tavern in the city.

Wijnand Fockink, Pijlsteeg 31, tel: (020) 639-2695. The inside of this tasting-house, which dates from as long ago as 1679, is decorated with an interesting collection of geniever bottles painted with the portraits of every mayor of the city since 1591.

Café In de Wildeman, Dam 11, tel: (020) 623-0815. Founded in 1690, this popular café offers patrons a range of 150 beers from all over the world. Unlike most of the taverns in Amsterdam, it also offers a non-smoking room.

Café 't Smalle, Egelantiersgracht 12, tel: (020) 623-9617. Restored to its original 18th-century condition approximately 20 years ago, this is one of the finest old-fashioned cafés in the city.

Outside the Centre

The area to the south and west of the Singelgracht and east of the River Amstel is a diner's desert, where restaurants, except for those in large hotels, are thin on the ground.

LUXURY

Sazanka Teppan Yaki and **Yamazoto**, Hotel Okura (*see* Where to Stay). Fine Japanese dining.

Le Ciel Bleu, Hotel Okura (*see* Where to Stay). French *haute cuisine*.

Gambrinus, Ferdinand Bolstraat 80, tel: (020) 671-7389. This French restaurant is rather expensive.

Chambertin, Hotel Apollofirst (*see* Where to Eat). Stylish *fin-de-siècle* restaurant with an attractive garden.

MID-RANGE

Ambrosia, Stadhouderskade 31, tel: (020) 664-0408. Caribbean-style restaurant where prices are reasonable.

NIGHTLIFE AND ENTERTAINMENT

Amsterdam is well-known as one of Europe's liveliest after-dark cities, with a choice of entertainment out of all proportion to its size, spanning everything from high culture to lowlife. Whether your tastes include opera, cinema, theatre, ballet, jazz, rock, blues, dance, trance or striptease, Amsterdam is able to pander to them every night of the week and virtually around the clock.

CASINOS

Holland Casino Amsterdam, 64 Max Euweplein, tel: (020) 620-1006.

CINEMAS

English-speaking cinema-goers are also in for a treat in Amsterdam, as almost all English-language films are shown undubbed (with Dutch subtitles) in the city's dozens of cinemas.

Amsterdam at a Glance

City, Kleine Gartman-plantsoen 15–19, tel: (020) 623-4579. Seven screens.
Desmet, Plantage Midden-laan 4, tel: (020) 627-3434. Mainly for a gay audience.
Tuschinski, Regulierbreestraat 26, tel: (020) 626-2633. Magnificent art-deco cinema with six screens; widest choice of English-language screenings in Amsterdam.

CLASSICAL MUSIC, OPERA AND BALLET

The Stadsschouwburg, the Concertgebouw, the Beurs van Berlage and the Muziektheater are on the international circuit for the world's leading orchestras and theatre companies. Rather than calling individual theatre box offices, make your bookings through **VVV** tourist offices or through the **AUB Ticket Shop**, Leidseplein 26, Mon–Sat 10:00–18:00, Thursday until 21:00 (personal callers only) or by telephone through the **AUB Uitlijn**, tel: (020) 621-1211.
Concertgebouw, 2–6 Concertgebouwplein, tel: (020) 671-8345. The venue for classical orchestral music by world-class performers.
Muziektheater, Amstel 3, tel: (020) 625-5455. Classical music, opera and ballet.
Stadsschouwburg, Leidseplein 26, tel: (020) 624-2311. Grand venue for classical music performances.

DISCOS AND DANCE CLUBS

Discos and dance clubs cater to all tastes, from middle-aged, middle-of-the-road disco music to the latest in trance and techno. The latest disco is **More**, in the former Roothanhuis building at Rozengracht 133. Gay nights on Wednesday, garage and two-step on Friday and DJs and other club nights through the week. Opened early in 2001, **Club Panama**, in a restored 19th-century ware-house, corner of Oostelijke Handelskade and Veemkade, features live concerts and a range of different music and DJs in different rooms.
Paradiso, 6–8 Wetering-schans, Leidseplein; programme and tickets from VVV Amsterdam Tourist Office. Amsterdam's mecca of modern music, in a former church. Fantastic acoustics, the best atmosphere in the city, one of the coolest places in Europe for 30 years. Best live music and dance nights in town. VIP Club on Fridays for techno, drum & bass, big beat and speedgarage. Paradiso, twice monthly on Saturday, for soul, funk and disco. Bassline, twice a month on Sundays, for hip-hop.
Arena Club, 's-Gravesand-straat 51. Full-service budget hotel (Europe's largest), café-restaurant and all-night party club. For tickets and information, contact VVV Amsterdam Tourist Office.

Gay and Lesbian Clubs
Amsterdam has a thriving gay nightlife scene. Venues, as ever, go in and out of fashion but there are lots of gay clubs in the Rembrandtsplein area. Look at *Time Out: Amsterdam*, the monthly listings magazine, for the latest places to go.

INTERNET CAFÉS

easyEverything, Reguliers-breestraat 22, open 24 hours. Huge full service cybercafé near Rembrandtplein. Website: www.easyEverything.com Other internet cafés include **The Internet Café**, Martelaars-gracht 11, tel: (020) 627-1052, and **Internet Freeworld Café**, Nieuwendijk 30, tel: (020) 620-0902, both open 09:00–00:00.

ROCK, JAZZ AND BLUES

Tourist nightlife centres around the **Leidseplein**, **Rembrandtsplein** and surrounding streets, where virtually every bar and café plays live music (rock, blues or jazz) after dark. Admission is free to most, but drinks are more expensive than in bars which don't offer live music. Amsterdam has far too many bars offering live music nightly to list exhaustively, but some recommended venues around the city include: **Pianobar le Maxim**, 35 Leidsekruisstraat, tel: (020) 624-1920. Easy-listening piano music, cocktail bar ambience.
Ciel Bleu Bar, Okura Hotel, 175 Ferdinand Bolstraat, tel:

Amsterdam at a Glance

678-7111. One of the city's better hotel cocktail bars.
Bamboo Bar, 66 Lange Leidsedwarsstraat, tel: 624-3993. Jazz and blues live.
Joseph Lam Jazz Café, 242 van Diemenstraat, tel: 622-3626. Specializes in Dixieland jazz, Friday–Sunday night only.
Melkweg, Lijnbaansgracht 234A, tel: (020) 624-1777. Venerable alternative music and performance venue founded in the 1960s and still going strong.

STRIPTEASE
The red light district, of course, offers its own brand of nightlife to those who want it.
Casa Rosso, Oudezijds Voorburgwal 106–108, tel: (020) 627-8954. Does its best to present erotica as good clean fun; at least they don't water the drinks and your wallet should be safe.

SHOPPING
Like all major European tourist cities, central Amsterdam is dominated by shops selling the tackiest of souvenirs. Some visitors may be surprised to find explicit pornography openly on sale next to postcards, camera film and T-shirts. However, Amsterdam also has some excellent shopping for art, antiques and curios, both in established galleries and auction rooms, and at the various regular markets around the city.

OUTDOOR MARKETS
These include the **Postzegelmarkt** (Stamp Market) along Nieuwezijds Voorburgwal, Wednesday and Saturday, 13:00–16:00.
Kunstmarkt (Art Market) on the Spui, April–November, Sunday 10:00–18:00.
Spui Boekenmarkt (Book Market), Friday 10:00–18:00.
The floating **Bloemenmarkt** (Flower Market), Monday–Saturday, 09:30–17:00.
Kunstmarkt (Art Market) at Thorbeckeplein, March–November, Sunday, 10:30–18:00.
Flea Market at Waterlooplein, Monday–Friday 09:00–17:00, Saturday 08:30–17:30.

INDOOR MARKETS
In the Jordaan area:
Antiquemarkt de Looier (Looier Antique Market), Elandsgracht 109, Saturday–Wednesday 11:00–17:00; Thursday 11:00–21:00.
Rommelmarkt (Flea Market), Looiersgracht 38, Saturday–Thursday 11:00–17:00.

ARTS AND ANTIQUES
Antique dealers and galleries cluster near the Rijksmuseum along the Spiegelgracht, a short canal lined by almost 100 antique shops. A full list is available from VVV Amsterdam Tourist Board.

CLOTHES
Stylish designer stores are to be found in the Oud Zuid (Old South) part of town. Beethovenstraat, Van Baerlestraat and PC Hoofstraat are the places to look for international designer names, fashionable boutiques, jewellers, exclusive shoe shops and accessories.

DUTY-FREE
Amsterdam Schiphol Airport has a very extensive duty-free shopping area; for a shopping catalogue write or fax. Dept SGE, PO Box 7501, 1118 ZG, Amsterdam Schiphol Airport, fax: (020) 601-2967.

DIAMONDS
Amsterdam is also a world diamond centre, and many of the city's diamond polishers offer free cutting demonstrations as well as sales of set and unset stones. Main outlets include:
Amsterdam Diamond Centre, 1 Rokin, tel: (020) 624-5787.
Bonebakker, 88–90 Rokin, tel: (020) 623-2294.
Coster Diamonds, 2–6 Paulus Potterstraat, tel: (020) 676-2222.
Gassan Diamonds, 173–175 Nieuwe Uilenburgerstraat, tel: (020) 622-5333.
Van Moppes and Zoon, 2–6 Albert Cuypstraat, tel: (020) 676-1242.
Principal Diamonds, 3 Tweede Weteringdwarstraat, tel: (020) 624-3417.
Rokin Diamonds, 12 Rokin, tel: (020) 624-7973.

Amsterdam at a Glance

Stoeltie Diamonds,
13–17 Wagenstraat,
tel: (020) 623-7601.

TOURS AND EXCURSIONS

A wide range of guided
tours and excursions within
Amsterdam and to neigh-
bouring parts of the
Netherlands is offered by
an equally wide range of
tour companies. Cycling
tours and canal cruising are
also offered. Half-day excursions can include trips to the
Zaanse Schans, a pretty
windmill village, and to
Volendam and **Marken**,
fishing villages on the
shores of the Ijsselmeer,
Delft, **The Hague** and
Scheveningen, as well as
the famous **Keukenhof
flower gardens** (April–May).
These gardens, situated near
Lisse, are one of the most
popular excursions from Amsterdam and can be reached
by train or bus. Open only in
spring, when you can see six
million tulips, narcissi,
daffodils and hyacinths in
full colourful glory.

Rijksmuseum, tel: (020)
673-2121.
Westerkerk, church office,
tel: (020) 612-6856.
Royal Palace, tel: (020)
620-4060.
Lindbergh Excursions,
Damrak 26, tel: (020) 622-
2766, fax: (020) 622-2769.
Coach tours, canal cruises,
guided walks, longer tours.

Keytours Holland, Dam 19,
tel: (020) 624-7304, fax:
(020) 623-5107. Coach
tours, canal cruises and
guided tours.
Yellow Bike, Nieuwezijds
Voorburgwal 66, tel: (020)
620-6940, fax: (020) 638-
2125. Organized bicycle
tours on the canals.
Walter M. G. Altena,
34I Pieter Lastmankade,
tel: (020) 662-9784,
fax: (020) 671-7916.
Guided city walks.

USEFUL CONTACTS

**VVV Amsterdam Tourist
Office** has offices within
Centraal Station (daily
09:00–17:00); immediately
outside Centraal Station
at Stationsplein 10 (daily
08:00–16:00); at Leidseplein
1 (daily 09:00–19:00); and
at Stadionplein (Mon–Sat
09:00–17:00); for central
information tel: 0900 400
4040, fax: (020) 625-2869,
daily 09:00–17:00.
Information, a range of maps
and leaflets, most with a
quite high cover price; guided
walks; tour and hotel bookings; public transport tickets
and museum cards.
**Amsterdam Schiphol
Airport**, tel: 0900 503 4050.
For flight enquiries and
arrivals information, tel:
(020) 474-7747.
**Central Medical and Dental
Service**, tel: 0900 503 2042.
Emergencies, tel: 06 11.
Police, tel: 06 11.

Police Headquarters,
117 Elandsgracht, tel: (020)
559 91 11.

LISTINGS

What's On In Amsterdam is
published in English every
three weeks by the VVV
Amsterdam Tourist Office
and contains information
on museums, exhibitions,
shopping, special events,
restaurants, nightlife and all
forms of nightlife as well as
lists of useful addresses and
telephone numbers. It can
be bought from VVV offices
and is given away by many
hotels. *Time Out: Amsterdam*,
the city's monthly English-
language arts and enter-
tainment magazine, carries
a full monthly agenda of
what's on in Amsterdam
and the Randstad.

EMBASSIES AND CONSULATES

Some consulates and
embassies are in Den Haag
(The Hague), diplomatic
capital of the Netherlands.
Dialling code from
Amsterdam is (070).
Australia: 12 Carnegielaan,
Den Haag, tel: 310-8200.
Canada: 7 Sophialaan, Den
Haag, tel: 361-4111.
Ireland: Dr Kuyperstraat 9,
Den Haag, tel: 363 09 93.
New Zealand: Mauritskade
25, Den Haag, tel: 346 93 24.
UK: 44 Koningslaan,
Amsterdam, tel: 676-4343.
USA: 19 Museumplein,
Amsterdam, tel: 575-5309.

Travel Tips

Tourist Information

The Netherlands Board of Tourism maintains overseas information offices in London, New York, Toronto and Sydney.

VVV Amsterdam Tourist Office has offices within **Centraal Station** (open daily 09:00–17:00); immediately outside Centraal Station at **Stationsplein 10** (daily 08:00–16:00); at **Leidseplein 1** (daily 09:00–19:00); and at **Stadionplein** (Mon–Sat 09:00–17:00).

For **central information** tel: 0900 400 4040, fax: (020) 625-2869, daily 09:00–17:00.

Other tourist offices include VVV **Den Haag**, Koningin Julianaplein 30, tel: 0900 340 3505, fax: (070) 347-2102; VVV **Rotterdam**, Coolsingel 67, tel: 0900 403 4065, fax: (010) 413-0124; VVV **Utrecht**, tel: 0900 414 1414, fax: (030) 233-1417; VVV **Haarlem**, Stationsplein 1, tel: 0900 616 1600, fax: (023) 340-537; VVV **Gouda**, Markt 27, tel: (01820) 13666, fax: (01820) 83210; VVV **Leiden**, Stationsplein 210, tel: (071) 146-846, fax: (071) 125-318;

VVV **Delft**, Markt 85, tel: (015) 126-100, fax: (015) 132824. All have the same opening times as the Amsterdam VVV offices.

Entry Requirements

Visas are not required for citizens of the EU countries nor for US, Canadian, Australian, New Zealand and South African citizens intending to stay for less than three months.

Customs

Normal European Union customs requirements apply. Those arriving from outside the EU may bring in the following quantities: 200 cigarettes or cigarillos or 50 cigars or 250 grams of tobacco, 1 litre of spirits or 2 litres of wine, 50cc of perfume, 500 grams of coffee or 100 grams of tea. There are no limits on the quantities of tax-paid goods which may be brough in from or taken out to other EU countries for personal use, but duty-free and tax-free goods are not available to those travelling between EU, including non-EU nationals.

Health Requirements

None.

Getting There

By air: Amsterdam Schiphol Airport (tel: 0900 503 4050) is 15km (9½ miles) from the city centre and is connected to the city by excellent road and rail links. Trains to Amsterdam Centraal Station leave four times an hour between 06:00 and 24:00 and hourly between 01:00 and 05:00; the journey takes about 25 minutes.

Direct trains from Schiphol also run to The Hague and Rotterdam; the journey takes less than an hour.

Schiphol is a major international airline hub, with Royal Dutch Airlines (KLM) and most other major carriers providing service to cities in North and South America, Africa, Asia and Australasia and to capitals and regional hubs throughout Europe.

By road: Amsterdam is on the European motorway network, with fast highways connecting it with other points in the Netherlands, Germany to the north and east and Belgium to the south.

By rail: The high-speed Thalys network, a joint venture between Dutch, Belgian and German railways, connects Amsterdam with Cologne and Düsseldorf in Germany and with Brussels and Paris. Thalys trains connect in Brussels with high-speed Eurostar services from London via the Channel Tunnel.

By boat: Ferry services connect Hoek van Holland, 90 minutes from Amsterdam by rail or two hours by road, with English North Sea ports including Sheerness and Harwich.

What to Pack

Everyday wear will depend on the season. Comfortable walking footwear, a shower-proof coat or jacket, a light sweater and a hat or umbrella are useful even in summer. From September until the end of April be prepared for cold, wet weather with sub-zero temperatures, snow and ice from November to March.

Money Matters

In 2001 the Dutch guilder was worth approximately UK£0.30/US$0.50. The Netherlands is among the European Union states which will adopt the single European currency, the euro, in 2002 when the guilder along with most other European currencies will cease to exist.

Changing money: GWK-Exchange, Centraal Station, tel: (020) 620-8121, open round the clock every day.

Change Express exchange offices are at 86 Damrak, tel: (020) 624-6682, 08:00–23:45

GOOD READING

• Banham, Reyner (1986) *Los Angeles: The Architecture of Four Ecologies*. Penguin.
• Schama, Simon (1988) *The Embarrassment of Riches*. Harper Collins, London.
• Gauldie, Robin (1996) *Walking Amsterdam*. New Holland, London.
• *The Golden Book of Amsterdam* (Bonechi)
• Bakker, B. (ed.) (1988) *Amsterdam: The History of the City*. Waanders.
• Fromentin, Eugène (1981) *The Masters of Past Time: Dutch and Flemish Painting from Van Eyck to Rembrandt*, Phaidon, London.
• *The Diary of Anne Frank* (1995) Macmillan, London.

---

daily; 150 Kalverstraat, tel: (020) 627-8087, 08:00–20:00 daily; 1 Leidseplein, tel: (020) 622-1425, 08:00–24:00 daily.

There are dozens of other exchange offices throughout the city, many of them charging very high commissions. Check the rate of exchange and the rate of commission before making a transaction.

Travellers cheques: all major travellers cheques and currencies can be exchanged at banks and bureaux de change.

Credit cards: all major credit cards are widely accepted.

Tipping: is not essential except in restaurants, where a 15% service charge is normally added to the bill.

Tax: Visitors from outside the European Union can reclaim value added tax on purchases costing more than 300 guilders in any one shop and exported within 30 days of purchase. Many shops display a conspicuous 'Tax Free for Tourists' logo and these will be pleased to help you with the tax reclaim formalities.

Accommodation

Amsterdam has a wide choice of accommodation, from five-star international chain hotels to cheap dormitories for budget travellers. At all levels rates are comparatively expensive

Booking a room: the Nederlands Reserverings Centrum (Netherlands Reservation Centre), an organization owned by Dutch hotel-owners, handles bookings free of charge for around 1700 classified hotels. The NRC works on a service basis, charging no fee to its members or their customers. Booking and confirmation is computerized and you can book by telephone, fax or by mail. The NRC also handles bookings for self-catering apartments and bungalows, as well as for the Holland Festival and other events in Amsterdam.

Netherlands Reservation Centre, PO Box 404, 2260 AK Leidschendam, Netherlands, tel: (070) 419-5500, fax: (070) 419-5519.

Local VVV tourist offices throughout the Netherlands have a national hotel booking system through which you can book a room not only locally but elsewhere in the Netherlands. The only snag is that you have to do it in person: telephone and fax bookings are not allowed. There is a small booking fee.

A high-tech Airport Information Panel at Schiphol International Airport arrival hall lists and illustrates hotels with accommodation available in categories from budget to deluxe in Amsterdam, Leiden and Utrecht. Reservations are made through a courtesy phone link and a built-in printer provides booking confirmation and details of how to reach the hotel.

Classification: hotels in the Netherlands are classified under the Benelux Hotel Classification scheme which also operates in the neighbouring countries of Belgium and Luxembourg. All properties are inspected every two years to ensure standards are met. The system places strong emphasis on safety and hotels failing to make the grade are declassified. A shield denoting the rating of each hotel is displayed prominently near the main entrance.

Accommodation in the Randstad Towns

Places to stay in The Hague, Rotterdam, or their smaller neighbours are available, though the range is generally not as wide as in Amsterdam. Really cheap budget accommodation at the one- or two-star level, in particular, is not so readily available. Be aware, too, that hotel beds are at a premium throughout the tourist summer season in smaller towns, and that Rotterdam and

---

PUBLIC HOLIDAYS AND FESTIVALS

1 January ●
New Year's Day
March/April (variable) ●
Good Friday, Easter Sunday and Monday
April 30 ●
Queen's Day, celebrating the royal birthday
5 May ●
Liberation Day
May (variable) ●
Whit Sunday and Monday, Ascension Day
25 and 26 December ●
Christmas Day and Boxing Day.

These are essentially family feast days with generally little public celebration.

The Hague are year-round business, conference and exhibition destinations where hotel rooms generally command a high price. It is advisable to make your accommodation arrangements before leaving Amsterdam, either through the VVV or NRC systems or through one of the many tour agencies in Amsterdam.

Eating Out

The choice of restaurants in the city centre reflects Amsterdam's ethnic mix and its position in the heart of Europe, with Tex-Mex, Argentinian and Chilean restaurants, Greek tavernas, German beer-cellars, Italian pizzerias and Turkish, Spanish, and Portuguese eating places. There are plenty of Middle Eastern – mainly Turkish and Lebanese – establishments as well as Far Eastern restaurants including Indonesian, Chinese and Japanese cuisine.

Amsterdam cannot claim to be among Europe's cheaper dining cities, but for those on a budget there are plenty of snack bars selling local favourites like pickled herring as well as imported snacks such as felafel, pizza and kebabs.

Eating out in the Randstad Towns

The heart of each of the smaller Randstad Towns is the medieval market square, known as the Markt. These pretty squares are conveniently lined with cafés and

---

CONVERSION CHART		
FROM	**TO**	**MULTIPLY BY**
Millimetres	Inches	0.0394
Metres	Yards	1.0936
Metres	Feet	3.281
Kilometres	Miles	0.6214
Square kilometres	Square miles	0.386
Hectares	Acres	2.471
Litres	Pints	1.760
Kilograms	Pounds	2.205
Tonnes	Tons	0.984

To convert Celsius to Fahrenheit: x 9 ÷ 5 + 32

restaurants, many of which offer outside tables in summer. You will also find basic fast-food outlets selling the usual Dutch snacks like meatballs, herring, burgers and french fries in and around each station concourse.

Throughout Amsterdam and the Netherlands, look out for the soup tureen logo of Stichting Neerlands Dis, an association of hotels which offer authentic Dutch regional dishes with a three-course meal at no more than Dfl 50 a head. Look out too for restaurants taking part in the Netherlands Board of Tourism's Tourist Menu scheme, which offer a three-course dinner at around Dfl 30 a head.

Transport

Air: Travelling by air within a country as small as the Netherlands is pointless. Distances are so short that rail travel is virtually always more convenient.
KLM CityHopper, tel: (020) 474-7747 operates flights between Amsterdam and Groningen in the north of the country and Maastricht in the south.
Rail and Bus: Trains leave frequently from Amsterdam Centraal Station, Stationsplein (open Monday–Friday 07:00–19:00, weekends 08:00–19:00, tel: 0900 92 92) for all the Randstad towns. Long-haul bus routes are also operated by Netherlands Railways; route and schedule information is available on the same number.

ROAD SIGNS

Street signs are found in the standardized format in use throughout Europe.
Many street signs, shop signs and directions are repeated in English. Some useful ones to learn include:
Niet roken ● No smoking
Gevaar/Let op/Pas op ●
Danger/look out/Beware
Toegang verboden ●
No entry
Vrij toegang ●
Free admission
Ingang ● Entrance
Uitgang ● Exit
Open ● Open
Gesloten ● Closed

Road: Car rental is not advised for exploring Dutch cities as distances are very short, parking is always a problem, and fines for illegal parking are heavy. However, for those wishing to explore further afield, car rental is available in the city centre and at Schiphol Airport.
Avis: 380 Nassaukade, tel: (020) 683-6061; Hogehilweg 7, tel: (020) 564-1611.
Europcar: 51/53 Overtoom, tel: (020) 683-2123; Schiphol, tel: (020) 316-4190.
Hertz: 333 Overtoom, tel: (020) 612-2441 ; Schiphol, tel: (020) 610-5416.

Driving licenses issued by other EU countries are valid. Non-EU visitors need an International Driving Licence, obtainable in the Netherlands or before you leave. When renting a car, full collision damage waiver and liability insurance is recommended. Drive on the right and observe

speed limits of 50 kph (30 mph) in towns, 80 kph (50 mph) on main roads and 120 kph (74 mph) on motorways. Rear seat and front seat passengers and drivers must wear seatbelts.

In an **emergency**, contact the Dutch motoring association ANWB from motorway emergency telephones or tel: 06 08 88.

Maps and motoring guides are available from all VVV tourist offices.
By foot: Many Amsterdam streets are pedestrianized, and all have separate cycle lanes. On non-pedestrianized streets, pedestrians should be especially alert for trams, which have right of way over everything and everybody, and cyclists. Both move silently, and often the first warning that they are almost upon you is the sound of an irritated ringing bell.

Business Hours

Banks and public offices open Mon–Fri 09:00–16:00. Shops open Mon–Sat 08:30–17:30. Some shops stay open late on Friday evening until 21:00.

Time Difference
GMT +1

Communications
The area dialling code for Amsterdam is (020) for calls from within the Netherlands and (00 31 20) for calls from abroad.
General Post Office, 250–256 Singel, tel: 556-3311, Mon–Fri 09:00–18:00, Sat 10:00–13:30.

Telecenter PTT Telecom
(phone, fax, telex and telegram services), 48 Raadhuisstraat, tel/fax: 626-3871, daily 08:00–02:00.
AT&T Netherlands, 733 Strawinskylaan, tel: 570-2100
AT&T USA direct service, tel: 06 0229111.

Electricity
Electrical supply is standard mainland European 220V AC. Plugs have two round pins.

Weights and Measures
The Netherlands uses the metric system.

Health Precautions
No special health precautions are required.

Health Services
Private and public medical services are readily available and are of a high standard. European Union residents holding an E111 certificate – available from your doctor or health department before departure – are entitled to free treatment.
Central Medical and Dental service, tel: 0900 503 2042.

Personal Safety
Amsterdam has a relatively low rate of violent crime but non-violent thefts from the cars, hotel rooms and pockets of unwary tourists are not uncommon. Police advice is to leave valuables and money in the safe of your hotel: and to carry no more money than you need.

USEFUL PHRASES			
ENGLISH	**DUTCH**	**ENGLISH**	**DUTCH**
Yes	Ja	Hospital	Zeekenhuis
No	Nee	Doctor	Dokter
Please	Astublieft	Bank	Bank
Thank you	Dank u/ bedankt	Toilet	Toeleten
		I come from...	Ik kom uit...
Sorry	Pardon	Where is...?	Waar is...?
Hello	Dag	1	een
Goodbye	Tot ziens	2	twee
Good morning	Goeiemorgen	3	drie
Good		4	vier
afternoon	Goeiemiddag	5	vijf
Good evening	Goedenavond	10	tien
Good night	Welterusten	50	vijftig
Left	Links	100	honderd
Right	Rechts	200	tweehonderd
When	Waneer	1000	duizend
Where	Waar	Monday	Maandag
How far to...	Hoe vaar naar...	Tuesday	Dinsdag
Station	Station	Wednesday	Woensdag
Hotel/	Hotel/	Thursday	Donderdag
Guesthouse	Pension	Friday	Vrijdag
Chemist	Apotiek	Saturday	Zaterdag
Post office	Postkantoor	Sunday	Zondag

Emergencies
General emergencies
(police, fire, ambulance): tel: 06 11.
Police: tel: 06 11.
Police Headquarters: 117 Elandsgracht, tel: 559 9111.

Etiquette
No special requirements or unusual local conventions.

Language
English is spoken fluently by almost everyone throughout Amsterdam and the Netherlands; English-language tourist information, maps, and restaurant menus are widely available. Though most letters in Dutch are pronounced as in English, there are several traps for the unwary. Vowels are lengthened, logically enough, by doubling them (as in centraal or nationaal), but some vowel combinations have unexpected results: *ui*, *ei* and *ij* are all pronounced to rhyme with 'eye'. In consonant combinations such as *kn*, each letter is pronounced as a separate sound. In Dutch, *v* is pronounced like an English *f* and *w* like an English *v*. Both *g*, *gh* and *ch* are pronounced like the *ch* in the Scots *loch* (which is why foreigners find it so hard to get their lips round Van Gogh). *J* is pronounced like *y* is in yesterday.